
"The only way to cover Washington these days is to think of it as the way Hollywood was in the thirties and forties. All the fantasy is now being made here. The White House is really the backlot of Twentieth Century-Fox, the Pentagon keeps making Warner Brothers war films, Congress is where they make MGM comedies, and HEW is where they keep remaking old Charlie Chaplin movies.

"There are no bad guys in Washington. There are only good guys doing bad things."

Fawcett Crest Books by
Art Buchwald:

Have I Ever Lied to You?
Son of the Great Society
And Then I Told the President
The Establishment Is Alive and Well in Washington

Getting High in Government Circles

Art Buchwald

A FAWCETT CREST BOOK

Fawcett Publications, Inc., Greenwich, Conn.

GETTING HIGH IN GOVERNMENT CIRCLES

A Fawcett Crest Book reprinted by arrangement with G. P.
Putnam's Sons.

Library of Congress Catalog Card Number: 76-158365

Selection of the Playboy Book Club, November 1971

Printed in the United States of America
September 1972

Contents

---

1. **Presidential Body Language**

   The Autumn White House   12
   The Greatest Column   14
   Presidential Body Language   15
   Former President Nixon   17
   Raw Meat on the Table   19
   Nixon Is Safe   21
   Happy Halloween!   23
   Working Within the System   24
   What Is Wrong?   26
   The Great Silent Majority   28
   Sit Tight Till You Hear from Me   30
   Men in the Middle   32
   Where Is Martha Calling From?   34
   "Keep Me Out of It"   36

2. **Media Rare**

   Talk-Show Trouble   40
   TV News   42
   Reporter with a Star   44
   First the Bible, Then Shakespeare   46

Civil Defense and Television   48
The Invention of TV   50
Rooting for Walter   52
The Shock of Recognition   54

3. The Naked Man

The Moon Is Down   58
White Rats Have All the Fun   59
Which Side Are You On?   61
The Naked Man   63
The Impossible Dream   65

4. Trouble in Paradise

The Cleanest Shirts in Town   70
What Tahitians Think   71
Mother Nature's Last Will   73
"Not One Ruble"   75
School for Luggage Handlers   77
Saint Ralph's in the Square   79
How to Run a Railroad   80
Who Needs Them?   82
The Wives of Commuters   84
Trouble in Paradise   85
Saving the Railroads   87
Earth Day   89
The New Breed   90
Japanese SST   92
South Pacific   94

5. The Great American Rat Race

Tough Christmas Holidays   98
Dinner for One   99

A Divorce Insurance Plan 101
The Henpecked Father 103
The Great American Rat Race 105

6. The Enemy Cow

The Big Poker Game 108
BULL (Bureau for Lethal Lodges) 110
Rice—The Ultimate Weapon 111
Schwartzkopf's War 113
The Science of Body Counts 115
Applebaum's Latest Plan 116
Plane Talk 118
The Enemy Cow 120

7. The Loved Ones

The Jobless Patriot 124
Why Success Spoils Government 125
  Grants
The Case Against Edelweiss 127
Public Library Enemy No. 1 129
Living on the Plantation 131
How to Spot an Undercover Agent 133
Easy Rider 134
Fitzgerald's Blunder 136
An Army That Listens 138
The Loved Ones 140

8. Midi uber Alles

Midi uber Alles 144
No Fun at the Fur Farm 146
Gung Ho 147
The Suit That Looked Like an Edsel 149

The Russians Are Coming   151

9. Virgin Power

Summer Campus Mail   156
Success Syndrome   157
The Dropouts   159
The New Lecture Scene   161
An Opening at the University   163
Degrees in Mass Transportation   165
The Black Brain-Drain   167
Recruiting Black Scholars   169
Virgin Power   170

10. How They Merged Santa Claus

Nobody Pays   174
Where Have All the Tipsters Gone?   176
Inflation and the Good Guys   178
A Nation of Banks   179
Hints for Tax Time   181
Fighting Inflation   183
Free Gifts for All   185
How They Merged Santa Claus   187
Before the Ax Falls   189
Canceling Insurance   190
Good-bye, Jones   192

11. Fun and Games

The Pro Football Murder Mystery   196
Summer Reading   198
For the Entire Family   200
Adult Movies   202
What Not to Say   204

Tahitian Women's Lib   205
Violence Is Taxable   207

12. Where Nixon Went Wrong

The Solution to Welfare   212
Income Tax Day   214
Children of Your Choice   216
Brother, Can You Spare $100?   218
It's Who Loses That Counts   219
The Don't Knows Are Riding High   221
Let's Pause for a Moment   223
Where Nixon Went Wrong   225
Women's Lib on Martha's Vineyard   227
Women's Liberation   228
Sex and the Washington Monument   230

13. And Nobody Laughed

The Computer Knows All   234
You Have to Have a Service   235
    Contract
The No-knock on the Door   237
Affluence Is No Fun   239
The Pothole Convention   240
Junk Instead of Junk Mail   242
The Great Data Famine   244
My Name's Howard   246
The Curse Is Working   247
On Buying a Flag   249
The New Game, Depression   251
Today Laos, Tomorrow . . .   253
And Nobody Laughed   255

1

PRESIDENTIAL BODY LANGUAGE

THE AUTUMN WHITE HOUSE

President Richard Nixon has just moved the White House from San Clemente, California, to Washington, D.C. The President indicated he might spend part of the winter in Washington, and he has asked his chief advisers and Cabinet officers if they would move there temporarily so he could confer with them.

When asked why the President had chosen D.C. for his fall headquarters, an administration spokesman said:

"The President has always had a warm spot in his heart for Washington, and with communications the way they are these days, it's just as easy for him to handle the nation's business from Washington as it is from San Clemente, California. Besides, if anything important happens, the President can always fly back to San Clemente."

While administration officials, for security reasons, refuse to discuss where the President will live, it is rumored that he has taken a house located at 1600 Pennsylvania Avenue, overlooking the Washington Monument on one side and Lafayette Park on the other. Neighbors in the area report that they have seen Secret Service men looking over the grounds and checking the neighborhood.

When a reporter asked the Nixon spokesman if the President would live in this particular house, the spokesman replied: "We are looking at several houses in Washington, and I believe it would be premature to say which one the President will live in."

The choice of Washington as the President's autumn White House came as a surprise to many residents of this sleepy town on the Potomac. The chamber of commerce was naturally delighted.

The man at the chamber office told me, "The fact that the President has selected Washington to live in this fall is a feather in our cap. It's going to bring in tourists and newspapermen, and we might even get to see some dignitaries from abroad. I guess you could say the President has put Washington on the map."

The manager of the town's largest department store said, "I don't know what effect the President's move here will have on business, but we do need a shot in the arm."

At the same time the chief of police said, "It could cause traffic problems, and I'm not sure I have enough men to handle it. But any time the President of the United States selects this place to live, even if it's for a short time, I think we should consider it an honor."

A neighbor of 1600 Pennsylvania Avenue didn't seem too pleased about the President's moving there. "We're quiet folks around here and we don't like to be bothered by a lot of commotion. Of course, the President has a right to live anywhere he wants, but I'm checking the zoning regulations just to make sure no one's violating any of the rules."

Another neighbor said, "It won't make no difference to me. Everyone's all excited about the President coming here, but I'm not going to change my way of life just because he wants to live in Washington for a while."

On the whole, the reaction to the President's moving to Washington has been good.

One high school student said, "I guess this will stop people from calling us a tank town."

One effect the news of the President's move has had is that hotelkeepers and restaurant owners have already raised their prices. While there has been some bitterness about this, one hotel owner said, "Heck, with the President in town we're going to have to put on more help. The people coming here to visit him are going to demand more service. We're not gouging anyone."

The real problem the people of Washington face is that they don't know how long the President is going to stay.

One merchant said, "We'll probably spend a lot of money fixing up the town, and then Mr. Nixon will decide to move on to someplace else. I know the President doesn't like to stay in one spot too long, and I think it's a mistake —just because he says he wants to live in Washington today—to assume that he still wants to make his headquarters here tomorrow."

THE GREATEST COLUMN

The President, whether he likes it or not, is the trend setter in this country, and when he speaks in superlatives, it is no surprise that everyone starts picking up the habit.

I imagine the first time we knew we had a President who pulls out all the stops was after our astronauts landed on the moon. The President was quoted as saying: "This is the greatest week in the history of the world since the Creation."

Then, before he gave his "State of the Union" speech, the President called it "the most comprehensive, the most far-reaching, the most bold program in the domestic field ever presented to an American Congress."

This kind of talk cannot but affect all American families.

For example, the other night, just as our family sat down to dinner, my wife announced, "I hope everyone has washed his hands because I have cooked the greatest meal ever served in the Western Hemisphere."

"That's good," I said, "because I've had the hardest day anyone has ever had since Gutenberg invented the printing press."

My fifteen-year-old daughter said, "We had the worst test in school today since the Spanish Inquisition."

"How did your football game go?" I asked my seventeen-year-old son.

"It was the most magnificent contest ever waged in intramural sport," he replied. "I made two of the most unbelievable catches in the history of the game."

"And what did you do today?" I asked my fourteen-year-old daughter.

"I had the greatest Coca-Cola I've ever drunk in my life."

My wife served the pot roast. "I hope everyone likes it because it's the most expensive pot roast my butcher has ever sold."

"It is truly delicious," I said. "And it explains why we

have the highest food bills of anyone on the Eastern Seaboard."

My wife took this as a personal criticism. "I can't help it if we're living in the highest inflationary period in modern times."

My son saved the day by asking, "Can I have the car tonight?"

"What for?" I asked.

"I'm going to the greatest movie ever made."

"What's the name of it?"

"I forget."

My fifteen-year-old daughter said, "Someone has to drive me to Jody's birthday party. It's supposed to be the grandest party ever given in the nation's capital."

My fourteen-year-old daughter said, "Then how come you were invited?"

My fifteen-year-old daughter said, "That's the most insulting thing anyone has ever said to me. You can take off my best blouse right now."

"Shut up," my wife said, "and eat your Brussels sprouts. I'm sick and tired of preparing the most fantastic meals ever served in this country and having vegetables left on the plates."

"Your mother is right," I said. "Besides, I hate to hear fighting during the most momentous banquet I have ever attended in this dining room."

My wife said, "After the most delicious apple pie anyone has ever tasted, I want everyone to help me with the largest pile of dirty dishes I've ever seen."

There were the loudest screams of protests ever uttered by an American family, but no one could escape.

Then we all went into the living room to watch President Nixon give his "State of the Union" speech which Attorney General John Mitchell described as "the most important document since they wrote the Constitution."

PRESIDENTIAL BODY LANGUAGE

There is a book called *Body Language* which deals with

the new science of kinesics, which is nonverbal communication. Julius Fast, the author, maintains that body gestures can tell more about a person than what he says. An unconscious movement, kinesics tells us, is all-revealing.

Fast is not the only person who is an expert on body language. My friend, Dr. Heinrich Applebaum, has been working on a project for some time to find out if President Nixon's gestures tell more about him than what he says.

Dr. Applebaum has been watching every TV program that President Nixon has appeared on and has come to some interesting conclusions.

"The President," Dr. Applebaum told me, "uses his body as well as anybody we've had in the White House. I have been able to interpret many of the gestures he makes."

"Could you give me an example?"

"Well, as you know, when he appears before large crowds he always raises his arms out and upward. Most people have felt he does this to acknowledge the cheers. But subconsciously he is at the floodgates trying to hold back the waves of inflation."

"That's very interesting."

"I have noted also that President Nixon is a fist clencher. When he's trying to make a point, he clenches his fist and moves his arm up and down."

"What could that mean?"

"It means that he subconsciously would like to sock somebody."

"I don't believe it."

"It's true. If you recall, in his TV appearance with John Chancellor, Eric Sevareid and Howard K. Smith the President was constantly clenching his fist. He started doing this after Howard K. Smith asked him what legal right did we have for being in Indochina, since the Gulf of Tonkin Resolution had been repealed."

"He didn't want to sock Howard K. Smith, did he?"

"No, stupid. He wanted to sock someone on his staff who hadn't prepared him for the question."

"What else?" I asked.

"The President is constantly using a karate chop when he's answering a question at a press conference. He keeps cutting the air with the flat of his hand."

"How do you explain it?"

"In 1962 the President said the press wouldn't have Nixon to kick around anymore. What he meant by that was he was going to take karate and make sure they didn't kick him. Naturally, as President, Mr. Nixon can't chop a reporter in the neck, so the gesture is symbolic of what he would like to do if he weren't in a position of responsibility.

"I notice the President wrings his hands a lot when he's speaking."

"Hand wringing is not uncommon for a President of the United States. I don't think you could put too much importance in President Nixon wringing his hands. But you could be concerned when he keeps his arms straight at his sides."

"What does that mean?"

"It means that no matter what he says, he doesn't plan to do anything about the problem."

"What does it mean when the President sits with his legs crossed?"

"It means he has a plan for getting us out of Vietnam, but he isn't going to tell us what it is."

FORMER PRESIDENT NIXON

"I would rather be a one-term President than a two-term President at the cost of seeing America become a second-rate power."—from President Nixon's speech to the nation on April 30, 1970.

"Good evening, ladies and gentlemen. I am Walter Cronkite, and today, May 12, 1973, I am sitting here in San Clemente, California, with former President Richard Nixon, who, as you know, decided not to run for a second term in 1972.

"Mr. President, you've been out of the White House for a few months now. How does it feel?"

"Well, Walter, I'd like to make one thing perfectly clear. I miss the White House as anyone who lived there does, but I have no regrets. As you know, I've joined the law firm of Agnew, Nixon, Mitchell, Haynsworth and Carswell, and we're doing very well."

"Mr. President, could you pinpoint the moment you decided not to run for another term?"

"I can't tell you the *exact* time. It could have been when John Lindsay defeated me in the primaries in New Hampshire. I decided at that time I would work for peace, and the only way I could do that was to eliminate myself as a Presidential contender. Besides, Pat didn't want me to run for another term."

"Mr. President, your decision to involve us in Cambodia has been interpreted by many as the reason that you could not run for a second term. Do you concur with this?"

"Well, I'd like to make this perfectly clear. I decided to go into Cambodia as a way of ending the war. Now, the Communists did not see it this way, and, therefore, they moved into northern Thailand. Then I was obligated to invade Thailand to clear out their supply bases there. After we did that, the Communists still refused to talk peace, and they started supplying northern Thailand from Burma. We couldn't allow them to use Burma as a dagger against our boys, so we launched the Burma offensive in hopes that Hanoi would see reason.

"Instead, the North Vietnamese started supplying Burma from Red China, so in order to protect our boys, we worked out a joint attack with the South Vietnamese on Red China.

"This strategy was approved by the Joint Chiefs of Staff, and I was only following out the policies of three Presidents: Eisenhower, Kennedy and Johnson."

"Why do you believe the Communist forces would never agree to peace?"

"Well, as you know, I was committed to withdrawing troops from Vietnam. The more troops I withdrew, the more military actions I approved. This proved a strain

18

on our armed forces. When we invaded China, I had only one hundred American soldiers left. When the aggressors didn't respond to our invasion at the Paris peace table, I had to ask the American people to send in a million more soldiers."

"And that was when you had the youth strike and every draftee in the United States refused to go."

"That's correct. That was in the fall of 1971. We had to jail 2,390,876 men for draft evasion.

"As you know, we didn't have enough jails to put everyone in, so I had to authorize an enormously expensive prison-building program. This money, which should have gone for military expenditures, caused inflation to spiral.

"So I made my decision to devalue the dollar, which caused the riots, which forced me to call out the troops, who, unfortunately, had no choice but to fire on the American protesters in the streets."

"Mr. President, what part do you think the students played in your decision not to run?"

(The following excerpts were eliminated from the program for security reasons at the request of Mr. Nixon.)

RAW MEAT ON THE TABLE

Probably the most misunderstood person in the Nixon administration is Vice President Spiro T. Agnew. Everyone believes that just because he attacks the press and TV media twice a week, Agnew is hostile to the communications people. But this is not the case. I have it from a reliable source that Agnew finds no pleasure in his work and is constantly hoping that the President will give him something *important* to do.

My source, who claimed to be so close to the Vice President that he had once been hit in the head by a volleyball Agnew was trying to serve, told me, "The Vice President is as upset as anybody about having to take after the Eastern establishment press in every speech."

"Then why does he do it?" I asked.

"*They* make him do it."

"Who does?"

"The Republican fund raisers. It's money in the bank."

"I don't understand."

"Well, take his speech in Houston last week. It was a five-hundred-dollar-a-plate dinner. When a guy shells out that kind of money, he doesn't want to hear the same old stuff about how well the President is doing with the war and the economy. The contributor knows that already. He wants some raw meat on that five-hundred-dollar plate."

"You mean Mr. Agnew is supposed to supply the raw meat?"

"Exactly. He has to get the juices flowing, or those people will just keep their hands in their pockets. Let us suppose you were a Texan and you had just paid one thousand dollars for your wife and yourself. What could possibly make a dinner of that kind worthwhile?"

"An attack on the New York *Times,* the Washington *Post* and the three television networks!"

"Of course. And, if you throw in the students and the professors for dessert, you've given those Texans a helluva meal."

"You can say that again," I said.

"It's no accident the Vice President always uses a Republican fund-raising dinner to take off on the communications media," he said.

"Why doesn't he attack the Democrats? Surely the Republicans would enjoy that?"

"Not half as much as they enjoy him knocking the media. The people in the White House who write his speeches know what raw meat works and what raw meat doesn't work at a fund raiser. One chunk out of CBS's hide is worth ten bites out of Senator Fulbright's."

"Then you mean all the Vice President is doing when he attacks the press is raising money for the Republicans?"

"Of course. Mr. Agnew loves the press. Some of his best friends are newspapermen. He reads the Washington *Post* and New York *Times* religiously every morning. You don't think he'd read those papers if he didn't like them.

He watches ABC, NBC and CBS every night. Surely he wouldn't watch the news on television if he thought it was slanted."

"I never thought of that."

"You must understand a Vice President's job is not an easy one. There isn't much for him to do, except raise money for his party."

"But isn't the Vice President finding it hard to say something new about the media after speaking to so many dinners?"

"He's finding it harder all the time. That's why in Houston he started to attack people by name, instead of just the publications they worked for."

"I noticed that," I said. "And I, frankly, was very disappointed."

"Why?"

"Well, if he was going to start attacking columnists by name, I was hoping he would do it alphabetically."

NIXON IS SAFE

Despite rumors that have been rampant in Washington in the past few months, I can now reliably report that Vice President Spiro Agnew has no intention of dumping Richard Nixon in 1972. A spokesman for the Vice President told me that Agnew was very satisfied with the job his President was doing and that he even intended to give him more responsibilities than any Vice President has ever given his President before.

The spokesman said, "I have been authorized to say that Vice President Agnew is proud of Mr. Nixon and feels the President has been a tremendous help to him in taking some of the Vice President's awesome burdens off his shoulders. Despite criticism of Mr. Nixon's speeches, Mr. Agnew has no intention of asking to see copies of them in advance."

"How does Mr. Agnew intend to make fuller use of his President?"

"The Vice President has urged the President to get more

exposure. For example, last week Mr. Agnew sent the President up to Capitol Hill to thank Congress for its support on the Vietnam issue. The Vice President has issued orders that President Nixon be briefed on every important decision that Mr. Agnew makes. He has made Mr. Nixon feel he is one of the family."

"But," I asked, "when President Nixon speaks out as he has been doing lately, is he speaking for himself or for the Agnew administration?"

"The Vice President sees Mr. Nixon's role as that of a missionary to explain the administration's policies and to seek support for them. The President fills a basic need, touching on subjects that the Vice President of the United States is in no position to discuss. Also, by turning over to President Nixon such day-to-day chores as Vietnam, disarmament, inflation, the urban crisis and the Middle East, the Vice President can devote himself to the important issues the country is interested in, such as moratoriums, students, snobs and intellectuals and the coverage of TV news."

"It has been bandied about that Mr. Agnew chose Mr. Nixon as his President to win the South. Is there any truth to this?"

"Absolutely none. Mr. Agnew chose Mr. Nixon because he considered him the best man for the job. Agnew's so-called Southern strategy has been made up by a handful of elite TV commentators who are prejudiced and opinionated. The Vice President is not interested in politics. His only concern is what is best for the country."

"Does it bother the Vice President that sometimes President Nixon gets bigger headlines than he does?"

"Never. Hubert Humphrey was always angered when President Johnson took the spotlight away from him, but Mr. Agnew feels there are enough headlines for everyone. Also, he believes that the more he gives President Nixon to do, the less the President will feel left out of things.

"The Vice President not only took Mr. Nixon with him to Cape Kennedy for the moon shot but made sure the President was seated next to him in the grandstand so Mr. Nixon could share some of the glory."

HAPPY HALLOWEEN!

It was Halloween, and all the pols were standing around the large iron kettle waiting for it to boil. Spiro, the chef, was adding some spices.

"A dash of nattering nabob, a cup of radiclib, and three tablespoonfuls of law and order."

Everyone clapped his hands. "Oh, this is going to be delicious," someone cried.

Chief Taster Dick took a wooden spoon and tasted it. "It's missing something."

He passed the wooden spoon around to his advisers. They all agreed, and sang together:

"It's missing something. It's missing something. Oh, what, oh, what is it missing?"

"I know," someone cried. "It's missing chopped rhetoric. No recipe is complete without chopped rhetoric."

"Of course," Spiro, the chef said. And he took a large box of rhetoric and poured the entire contents in.

Someone threw some wood on the fire and the brew started to bubble.

Chief Taster Dick took his wooden spoon and everyone held his breath. Dick made a face. "It's flat. It needs more Democrats."

Everyone joined hands and danced around the kettle chanting, "It needs more Democrats! It needs more Democrats!"

Spiro, the chef, finally said, "We've thrown in all the Democrats. We have none left."

They all cried in despair: "We have no Democrats left. We have no Democrats left."

"Oh, what should we do? Oh, what should we do?"

Chief Taster Dick stared at the pot. "Start throwing in Republicans."

There was a gasp from the witches. "Republicans?"

"That's what I said," Chief Taster Dick said.

Spiro, the chef, and three of the witches grabbed Charlie Goodell and threw him in the pot.

Goodell screamed and thrashed around as everyone clapped his hands and sang: "Charlie Goodell is stewing in the pot. Charlie Goodell is stewing in the pot. Poor old Charlie's stewing in the pot as Buckley marches on."

Spiro, the chef, stirred and stirred, and then he gave the spoon to Chief Taster Dick.

"That's better," he said, smacking his lips. "But it still needs another Republican."

"Another Republican?" everyone gasped.

"Throw in Lindsay," cried a goblin named Martha.

"Lindsay, Lindsay," everyone yelled. "The stew needs some Lindsay."

They heaved in Lindsay and added water to the pot.

Spiro stirred and seasoned it with a bowl of pornography, a pan of marijuana, a handful of media and a gravy of student unrest.

The pot was really boiling and everyone was licking his chops.

"Has there ever been a political brew like this?" cried one of the elves.

Chief Taster Dick went back to the pot and stuck his spoon in. Everyone watched.

"It's almost perfect. All it needs is a little more extract of fear."

Spiro added several gallons of fear, and then Chief Taster Dick smacked his lips and said one word: "Perfect."

They all clapped and cried, "Let us taste it! Let us taste it!"

But Spiro, the chef, slapped their hands with the spoon and said angrily, "Nobody gets to eat unless they pay two hundred and fifty dollars a plate."

WORKING WITHIN THE SYSTEM

For years now, our Congressmen on Capitol Hill have been urging students to "work within the system." You can imagine their surprise and consternation when the students took them up on it.

Congressman Halyard Hoakum was just putting some balls in his golf bag when his secretary came in and said, "Sir, there's a delegation of students outside from your district, and they want to see you."

Congressman Hoakum said, "For heaven's sake, it's Friday. Don't they know we don't work on Friday?"

"I told them that, but they still insisted on seeing you. They said they're from Fairweather State, your alma mater."

"All right, show them in," Congressman Hoakum said, "but be sure and interrupt me in twenty minutes. You can say the White House is calling."

The secretary showed ten students in.

Congressman Hoakum stuck his hand out. "Well, this is a great honor . . . a great honor. How's everything at Fairweather State?"

A young girl said, "Congressman Hoakum, we've come to discuss with you what is going on in Vietnam."

Congressman Hoakum said, "Of course you have. Say, let's pose for a photo together." He buzzed his pressman. "Jack, you want to bring in the camera and take some shots of me talking to a group of fine, dedicated Americans from Fairweather State? We could airmail it out there for Monday morning's papers. Good."

Jack came in with his camera.

Congressman Hoakum said, "Now gather around the desk here and pretend like you have something really serious to say."

"We *do* have something serious to say," a boy said. "Congressman Hoakum, the students at Fairweather State are concerned over the way the President has been—"

"Say, how's the football team going to be?" the Congressman asked. "Coach Fogel told me he might get a bowl invitation this year."

A girl pursued the subject. "We are fed up with rhetoric and pablum. We want our Representatives in Congress to do something."

"I know exactly how you feel," Congressman Hoakum

25

said. "When I was a student, I felt the same way. I said, 'Why can't we change things?' But since I've been in public life, I've taken a more realistic view. But you're too young to know that, and I envy your idealism. If I were your age, I'd be doing the same thing you're doing."

"How can we change things, Congressman Hoakum?"

"By working through the system . . . that's the American way. Our government with its checks and balances provides for everyone to have a voice in this country. And no one believes in the right of peaceful dissent more than I do. You getting all this on tape, Jack?"

"Congressman Hoakum," the girl spokesman said, "you have been a great help to us and have shown us what we have to do."

"It's wonderful that we can still communicate. What are you going to do?"

"We're going to get all the students at Fairweather State to work for your defeat in November."

Congressman Hoakum shouted, "You can't do that. I've been in Congress for twenty years."

"We'll see that it's your last one."

"Get out, you Commies," Hoakum yelled.

"You're all a bunch of rotten bums."

The students marched out singing. Hoakum, his head in his hands, said to his press man, "Jack, call J. Edgar Hoover and tell him to find the s.o.b. who's trying to get the kids to work within the system."

WHAT IS WRONG?

People who have been wondering why things have been unraveling so badly in Washington these days may be interested in the explanation of a distinguished Chinese scholar who visited the Capitol recently. Dr. Chun Ling is an expert in Feng Sui, otherwise known as the study of things in relation to where they are placed.

"Americans," Dr. Chun Ling said, "do not put much significance into what is in good harmony and bad harmony, but if buildings are not in harmony with each other, it is impossible for people to be in harmony."

Dr. Chun Ling said that the most striking example of this could be illustrated by the fact that the White House faces north and the Capitol of the nation faces east, and both have their backs to the Washington Monument. When buildings face in different directions, they do not have common goals.

"The Supreme Court faces Lincoln and that is good, but Lincoln from his monument must look at the back of the Senate and House of Representatives, and this is bad."

Dr. Chun Ling also said, "It is very sad the President's office is located in the west wing of the White House, because this puts him on the side of the Pentagon and away from Health, Education, and Welfare."

The Feng Sui expert said it is no accident that the Pentagon is as strong as it is in Washington. "The Pentagon is much larger than the Capitol and White House, and the two smaller buildings cannot control the bigger one. Not only that, but the Pentagon has too many faces and too many entrances directed in all directions. This multi-faceted design has forced the Pentagon to get involved in every direction it faces."

Dr. Chun Ling pointed something out to me that I had never noticed before, which shows you how important the study of Feng Sui can be.

"The Pentagon is across the Potomac River, and that is why the State Department, Capitol and even the White House have no control over it."

One of the most interesting things that Dr. Chun Ling said was that because the White House faces north, it looks on Lafayette Park. In the center of Lafayette Park is the Jackson Memorial, consisting of four giant antique guns. These guns have dominated every recent President's thinking. When the President is trying to think, it's inevitable that the guns in Lafayette Park can suggest military solutions to world problems. Dr. Chun Ling believes the guns should be removed at once and replaced with flowers.

When studying the science of Feng Sui, Dr. Chun Ling says that it is very important to know on what axis our

27

nation's leaders sleep. If they don't sleep on the same geographic poles, they can disrupt the flow of the earth's magnetism.

I had my doubts about Dr. Chun Ling's last statement, and so I did some Feng Sui research on my own. It appeared there was a lot to what he said. For example, I discovered that Senator Fulbright sleeps south to north and Martha Mitchell sleeps west to east. This is why they have never been able to see eye to eye on anything.

Vice President Agnew, on the other hand, sleeps south by southeast. Most Eastern establishment newspapermen and commentators sleep north by northeast. This, and only this, is what is causing the disharmony between the Vice President and the press.

I tried to find out in what direction President Nixon sleeps to make my study complete, but Ron Ziegler, his press secretary, told me emphatically, "The President never sleeps."

THE GREAT SILENT MAJORITY

Sometimes my friend Vladimar Kalinsky at the Soviet Embassy can drive me straight up the wall. The other day at lunch we got into an argument over the stupidest thing.

I was talking about President Nixon's great silent majority in the United States, and Kalinsky said, "The Soviet Union has a GREATER silent majority than the United States."

I immediately saw red. "How can you say that, Kalinsky? Everyone knows the United States has the greatest silent majority in the world."

Kalinsky knocked over his vodka glass. "The Soviets invented the silent majority," he shouted.

"Maybe so," I said, "but we have refined it. Thanks to American know-how, our silent majority is twice as silent as your silent majority."

"We had a silent majority in Russia before you knew

what a silent majority was," Kalinsky said. "Stalin was the father of the silent majority."

"Aha, but Stalin is gone and our silent majority is with us," I said. "Do you know that, according to the last Gallup Poll, our silent majority now comprises seventy-nine percent of the American people?"

Kalinsky sneered. "Our silent majority behind the Iron Curtain is ninety-nine percent, if you don't count Czechoslovakia."

"You're lying," I said.

Kalinsky took out a paper. "Here, look at the Harrowvitch Poll just taken in Moscow. Ninety-nine percent of all the people interviewed say they support Premier Kosygin's policy, which is to seek an honorable solution in Prague."

"Why don't you take the same poll in Siberia?" I asked Kalinsky.

Kalinsky choked on a piece of black bread. "You have no reason to insult me just because I have proof that the Soviet Union has a greater silent majority than the United States."

"Kalinsky, you do not fool me. Your silent majority is afraid to speak out; our silent majority has been heard from. Did you see all those telegrams on President Nixon's desk after his speech?"

"You call that a silent majority? There weren't enough telegrams on his desk to make it a silent majority," Kalinsky roared. "Have you ever seen a demonstration in Red Square? That's a silent majority."

"Our silent majority doesn't have to demonstrate," I said. "President Nixon knows they're out there."

"We have proven in the Soviet Union that our silent majority exists. But we have no proof that you even have a silent majority, except for Nixon's word."

"That's dangerous thinking, Kalinsky. If we ever unleashed our silent majority against your silent majority, we would wipe you from the face of the earth."

"Do not provoke us too far," Kalinsky said threateningly. "We have silent majorities stockpiled all over our country. You may knock out some of them, but your silent majority will take heavy casualties."

"Let's not argue, Kalinsky," I pleaded. "I admit the Soviet Union has a great silent majority. Will you admit we have a great silent majority, too?"

"I will admit you have a good silent majority, but not a great one—at least nothing comparable to what we've had for the last fifty years."

"You have insulted the President of the United States, Kalinsky," I said, getting up. "And I will not sit here and eat with you anymore."

SIT TIGHT TILL YOU HEAR FROM ME

There was a time when every Cabinet member of the Nixon administration was fighting to get in to see the President at the White House.

But after Secretary Walter Hickel was granted an audience with Mr. Nixon and fired on the spot, other Cabinet officers have decided there is no need to see the President after all.

Six months ago there were three or four Cabinet officers waiting in line by the White House gate, hoping to get a glimpse of the President, just so they could go back to their departments and say they saw him.

But all this has changed.

The other day a Cabinet officer I know received a telephone call from the White House. His wife answered.

"It's John Ehrlichman. He says you asked a year ago to see the President, and he thinks he can squeeze you in on Thursday between four and five."

"Oh, no," the Cabinet officer cried. "Tell him I changed my mind."

His wife transmitted the message and then told her husband, "He says even if you don't want to see the President, the President wants to see you."

"Tell him I've got to address a chamber of commerce meeting in Oklahoma on Thursday between four and five."

The wife did this and listened. "Yes, all right, we'll be there." And she hung up.

"Where will we be?" the Cabinet officer asked in fear.

"We've been invited to church services at the White House on Sunday," his wife said.

"Call back and tell him we don't believe in God," the Cabinet officer implored.

"Now stop being ridiculous. Surely if the President was going to fire you, he wouldn't do it at church services on Sunday morning."

"You don't know how those people operate over there at the White House. Two weeks ago they canned six poverty lawyers while the choir was singing 'Nearer My God to Thee.'"

"Well, you can't very well refuse an invitation to go to church services at the White House. Besides, if we sit in the back, maybe the President won't see us."

"All right, but let's pack and put our stuff in the trunk of the car, just in case," he said.

The Cabinet officer and his wife showed up at the White House the next Sunday. Billy Graham was reading from the Book of Job:

Why then did you bring me forth from the womb?
I should have died and no eye have seen me.
I should be as though I never lived;
I should have been taken from the womb to the grave.

The Cabinet officer whispered, "There, what did I tell you!"

"The message could be for the Secretary of the Treasury," his wife whispered back.

They looked around the room and saw other Cabinet officers whispering to their wives.

Billy Graham continued:

Are not the days of my life few?
Let me alone that I might recover a little
Before I go from whence I shall not return, to the
Land of darkness and gloom,

The black disordered land
Where darkness is the only light.

The Cabinet officer said, "It's either Romney or me."

Attorney General John Mitchell started passing the collection plate. As he handed the basket to the Cabinet officer he said quietly, "Sit tight until you hear from me."

But as the choir sang "Glorious Things of Thee Are Spoken," a task force from the White House had already taken over the Cabinet member's office and changed all the locks on the doors.

MEN IN THE MIDDLE

My friend Brightfelder is having an identity crisis. He said that no matter where he stood on the major issues in the United States today, he found himself in trouble.

"The fact that I'm against the bombing of New York buildings, the student takeovers of offices and intimidation by militant know-nothings makes me a Fascist pig."

"Well, there's nothing wrong with that," I said.

"Except that I think Spiro Agnew is full of hot air."

"But that makes you an effete snob and a pseudo-intellectual," I said.

"Exactly. I think Judge Julius Hoffman of Chicago is one of the great disasters of our judicial system."

"That makes you an ultra-left-wing revolutionary."

"At the same time, I think the Chicago Seven are a bunch of clowns who belong on the comic pages of the newspapers."

"Which makes you an apologist for the stinking bourgeois establishment."

"To my mind, Attorney General Mitchell would do anything to violate my constitutional rights in the name of law and order, and this makes me a limousine liberal."

"They're the worst kind."

"At the same time, I think we should beef up our police forces."

"Join the silent majority."

"I believe Nixon's Southern strategy is tearing this country apart."

"This makes you a typical Northern bleeding-heart hypocrite."

"At the same time the blacks call me a honky racist for not giving them my church."

"You seem to be all things to all men."

"I keep saying we should get out of Vietnam as fast as possible, and they call me a yellow neo-isolationist. But because I'm not willing to pull the troops out today, my left-wing pals say I'm a prize dupe of the military-industrial complex."

"How do you feel about the economy?"

"I'm against a recession which makes me a reckless Socialist free spender."

"What about inflation?"

"I'm against that too, for which I've been called a Nazi conservative who doesn't give a damn about unemployment."

"Any thoughts on the ABM?"

"It's a disaster and as phony as anything the Defense Department has come up with."

"But that means you're giving aid and comfort to the Commies."

"I'm the original pinko dove. And because I think the draft is safer for the country than a professional Army, my kid's friends refer to me as the 'war criminal.' "

"You have to have a strong hide to take all this name calling."

"The tragedy of all this is that the radical right knows exactly where it stands, and the radical left is completely secure in the knowledge it's right. But the Fascist pig, pseudo-intellectual effete snob of the radical middle is being torn apart."

"You can say that again," I said.

"Any country where a citizen has to choose between Judge Julius Hoffman and Yippie Abbie Hoffman is really in trouble."

WHERE IS MARTHA CALLING FROM?

All Washington is talking about Martha Mitchell. It isn't a question of what she is going to say, as there are no surprises in *that* anymore.

The big question that everyone is wondering about is: From where is she going to make her next telephone call? As everyone knows, Mrs. Mitchell is always calling the press at some unearthly hour in the night, but she doesn't want her husband, John, to hear what she's saying.

At first it was revealed she was making her calls from the bathroom. Then, when she called a UPI reporter, she said she was speaking from the balcony of her Watergate apartment.

No one knows where Martha Mitchell's next call is coming from.

Perhaps I can speculate.

"Hello, is this United Press? This is Martha Mitchell . . . I'm calling from my shoe closet, and I have to speak fast because my heels are killing me . . . I just thought you'd like to know what I think of that turncoat, John Lindsay. I think he should be hung by his fingernails . . . Yes, and that goes for Charles Goodell . . . Ouch! I just sat on a shoe tree . . . Yes, and they should both be crucified and be thrown out of the Republican Party . . . Listen, I have to go now . . . a hatbox just fell on me and I think I woke up John. Toodle-oo."

Three days later:

In a whisper. "Hello . . . *Life* magazine, this is Martha Mitchell . . . I'd like to blast Senator Gore . . . Can you put me in touch with someone who would be interested? . . . Thank you . . . Hello, hello. This is Martha . . . no, I can't speak louder. I'm calling from under the bed . . . John doesn't know I had an extension put in under here . . . He tore out the one I had in the bathroom . . . It's a tight squeeze under here . . . I just want to say that Senator Gore is despicable, and I hope the voters of Tennessee see that he never comes back to Washington . . .

Wait a minute, I think I heard John turn over . . . It's all right now . . . Gore is a terrible man and. . . ."

A week later:

"Hello, operator, get me the Arkansas *Gazette* . . . This is Martha Mitchell . . . No, I'm speaking as loud as I can . . . We're having a party here and I'm talking from the chandelier . . . That's right . . . the chandelier . . . Of course it's safe . . . The telephone company would not have put a line in up here if it weren't . . . I would like to talk to you about that rat, William Fulbright . . . What have you people done about him lately? How can you allow that ghastly man to stay in the Senate? He makes me sick . . . Oh-oh, the chandelier is starting to swing . . . Oh, dear, it's rocking . . . I better call you back. . . ! Owwwwww!"

A week later:

"Hello, give me Mike Wallace at CBS . . . Mike, this is Martha . . . What do you mean you're getting an echo? . . . Oh, I know why . . . I'm speaking in the dumbwaiter at the Watergate . . . Well, it's not very funny, Mike . . . It's uncomfortable as hell. But John found all my other extensions and I have to call from *somewhere* . . . Mike, what I called about is I thought you might want to do a program blasting the Supreme Court . . . Wait a minute, Mike . . . Someone on the third floor is ringing for the dumbwaiter . . .

"Oh, Mike, Mike, I'm stuck . . . I can't get out . . . I'm going down . . . Oh, dear, I'm not certain the extension cord is long enough . . . Mike, listen, if we get cut off, I think you should do an exposé of that awful William Douglas . . . Now someone on the sixth floor is ringing for the dumbwaiter . . . I don't know how I'm going to get back to my apartment . . . Mike, call my cook on the other line and ask her to ring for the dumbwaiter so I can get back to my own apartment. But tell her, for heaven's sakes, not to tell John where I am."

"KEEP ME OUT OF IT"

As everyone knows, there is a "new" Nixon and an "old" Nixon. For the past two years, the "new" Nixon is the one who has appeared on TV and at press conferences, and the "old" Nixon has stayed in the background.

The only time the "old" Nixon was allowed to make a public appearance was at the Pentagon, when he called the students "bums." This so infuriated the "new" Nixon that he ordered the "old" Nixon to remain out of sight. But this doesn't mean the "old" Nixon and the "new" Nixon are not still close friends.

For example, when the "new" Nixon came back from his earth-shaking trip to Europe, the first person he checked in with was the "old" Nixon.

"What's been happening since I've been gone?" the "new" Nixon asked.

"We're doing great, Dick," the "old" Nixon said. "I got Spiro to attack the campus unrest report and call the whole thing a fraud."

"Great," said the "new" Nixon. "You kept me out of it, I hope?"

"Of course, Dick. Now that Spiro's pulled the rug out from under the Scranton commission, you can say anything you want to about it and people won't care."

"Fine. What else?"

"Well, we really socked it to the pornography commission. Spiro has the country believing the Democrats are responsible for all the dirty movies and books in the United States."

"I like it," the "new" Nixon said. "But you kept me out of it?"

"They can't touch you. Every time someone starts screaming about Spiro's rhetoric, we say he's only speaking for himself. Then we leak it later that he's really speaking for *you*. We have the best of both worlds."

"Good thinking," the "new" Nixon said. "I don't know how I'd get along without the both of you."

"You should see Spiro, Dick. He's better at demagoguing than I ever was," the "old" Nixon said. "He learns fast, and I've never known a guy who enjoyed going for the jugular as much as he does."

"As long as he keeps me out of it," the "new" Nixon said.

"He uses words that no one's even heard of, and still gets standing ovations. The press can't get enough of him. And the money, Dick, it just keeps pouring in. Every time he says 'Doctor Spock,' we raise another hundred thousand dollars."

"Fine. What's going on politically around here?"

"You're going to love this, Dick. Agnew attacked Charlie Goodell, who's running for Senator in New York."

"Did he keep me out of it?" the "new" Nixon asked.

"Yep. He said Goodell was a radical lib, and he practically endorsed James Buckley of the Conservative Party."

"I hope people don't think I was behind it," the "new" Nixon said.

"You're clean, Dicky, absolutely clean. Only you and I know how much you wanted to zap Goodell. It also puts egg on Rockefeller's face, which I'm sure doesn't shake you up."

"As long as no one connects me with it. Hey, by the way, did you see the TV pictures of me riding in the rain with Tito?"

"No, I haven't had a chance to watch TV. I've been spending all my time with Spiro trying to think of new ways of attacking college administrators."

The "new" Nixon nodded his head. "I hope nobody thinks I have anything to do with it."

2

MEDIA RARE

TALK-SHOW TROUBLE

The United States is suffering from its worst shortage of radio and TV talk-show guests in twenty years. The reason for this is that while talk shows have been multiplying by the thousands, the people who have been appearing on them have become worn out. In 1960 there were 250 guests available for each talk show. Ten years later, there were 250 talk shows fighting over the same guests.

Things have gotten so bad that a professor who wrote a book about the mating habits of woodworms was recently kidnapped in front of the *Today* show in New York and flown out to California, where he was forced to go on a radiotelephone talk show instead.

Two famous late-night show hosts got into a fist fight in a Sixth Avenue delicatessen last month over a waiter who could make a white napkin look like a rabbit.

And only three weeks ago, two female talk-show hostesses had a hair-pulling contest in a beauty shop over the TV rights to an author of a definitive book on false eyelashes.

In order to avoid an all-out war between the talk-show commentators, a secret conference was called at Johnny Carson's hideaway farm in the Adirondacks.

Black limousines, with their shades drawn, kept arriving at two-minute intervals, and out stepped such big guns in the talk business as David Frost, Dick Cavett, Mike Douglas, Hugh Downs, Barbara Walters, Virginia Graham, Irv Kup and David Susskind. Every major TV host and hostess was there.

Everyone brought his own producer and talent coordinator for protection, but Carson's people made everybody leave their teleprompters at the door.

Ed McMahon opened the meeting by saying, "And heeerrrrre's Johnny."

Carson got down to business right away. "We all know why we're here," he said. "There's a crisis in the talk-show

40

business, and unless we find an answer to it, we'll all be doing commercials for Maxwell House coffee."

"Right," said Mike Douglas. "Now, my boys in Philadelphia say that unless some equal way is figured out to share the few available guests left, we're going to take them off the metroliner before they reach New York."

"Is that so?" said Virginia Graham. "Well, we on the West Coast are getting sick and tired of your Eastern talk shows coming out here and grabbing all our guests."

"That's right, Ginny," said Merv Griffin. "If you muscle in on our territory, we'll muscle in on yours."

David Frost spoke up, "We're not getting anywhere with threats. As I see it, no matter what we do, we've used up every singer, comedian, author and politician for the next two years. A new crop should be coming up by then, but none of us can wait. What I suggest is that we each volunteer to go on each other's shows to fill the vacuum. After all, we are more interesting than the people we interview."

"I agree with David," Dick Cavett said, "but it seems to me the public would become very suspicious if we kept turning up on each other's shows without a reason."

"Why don't we each write a book? Then we would have a legitimate reason for going on each other's show," David Susskind said.

Carson replied, "You know we don't have time to write books."

"But suppose," said Frost, "we put together transcripts of our interviews with our former talk-show guests. Wouldn't that constitute a book?"

"Of course," said Barbara Walters. "Then no one could criticize us for going on each other's show."

And so it was decided that each talk-show host would put together the best talks he or she has had. This would mean 345 books, which would take up the talk lack for the next two years.

As the long black limousines pulled out of Carson's farm the state police, who were tipped off to the meeting, showed up. But, unfortunately, almost everyone got away.

TV NEWS

The networks have all reexamined their news policies, as requested by the administration, and here is the result.

"Direct from our newsroom here in the White House is the evening news with Ronald Ziegler and Herb Klein in Washington, Strom Thurmond in Athens, Georgia, and Ronald Reagan in Sacramento, California. And here is Ron Ziegler."

"Good evening, ladies and gentlemen. All was peaceful and tranquil at the White House today. President Nixon worked in his office conferring with advisers and visitors. The President lunched with Mrs. Nixon and took a walk in the rose garden, stopping to talk with a six-year-old boy who was poking his head through the fence. The boy, whose name was Michael Redfern, of Boise, Idaho, told the President he was a member of the silent majority and supported his efforts to find a just and honorable solution to the war in Vietnam and that he was proud of the job the President was doing. The President was so pleased he presented Michael with a meat-loaf sandwich. And now to Herb Klein in the Executive Building."

"Thank you, Ron. The latest Gallup Poll has just revealed that ninety-eight percent of the people support President Nixon's domestic policies. This was two points up from last month when the President's popularity sagged momentarily, when milk was raised to one dollar a quart. And now to John Volpe at the Department of Transportation."

"Administration officials said they were terribly pleased with the progress being made on the SST airplane. In a test yesterday only seven thousand windows were broken in Boston, as opposed to previous tests when ten thousand windows were shattered in Providence, Rhode Island. Engineers hope to have all the bugs worked out of the SST by 1987, at which time the costs, now running at four billion dollars, will start going down.

"There was more integration in the South this week, and

for that story we go to Strom Thurmond in Athens, Georgia."

"Despite Justice Department pleas to give the school boards more time to work out a reasonable plan, two black children were admitted to a school in Mississippi yesterday. The integration took place peacefully and without violence, and administration officials said they were very pleased. The institution admitting the black students was the Mountain Valley School for the Blind. And now to Atlanta, Georgia, and our correspondent, John Mitchell."

"Thanks, Strom. Lester Maddox entertained leaders of the Republican Party at a picnic on the state house steps today and as an added treat sang 'God Bless America.' The Republicans denied that this had anything to do with the so-called Southern strategy of the party, but admitted they asked ex-restaurateur Maddox to cater the 1972 Republican Convention and serve fried chicken.

"Unruly students demonstrate in California. For that story we go to Ronald Reagan in Sacramento."

"Unruly students, most of them with beards and long hair, demonstrated today when the board of regents ruled that anyone protesting anything in California would automatically lose his driver's license. Six crop-dusting airplanes carrying a mixture of DDT and tear gas were used to break up the mobs, which were then strafed by fighter planes from the California National Guard. And now back to Ron Ziegler in the White House."

"Thank you, Governor. President Nixon was asked today at an impromptu press conference whether he supported Vice President Spiro Agnew's plan to withhold Social Security from anyone over sixty-five criticizing the administration and living within the geographical confines of New York or Washington, D.C. The President said he was aware of the speech but had no comment. And that's the way it is. This is Ron Ziegler saying good night."

REPORTER WITH A STAR

Attorney General John Mitchell backtracked slightly in the Justice Department's desire to use TV, magazine and newspaper reporters as deputies in the fight against crime. Before the Attorney General's statement, the Justice Department was handing out blanket subpoenas demanding that the networks, TV stations, magazines and newspapers turn over their unused film, photographs and even newspaper reporters' notebooks to be used as evidence in court.

While the news media feel threatened by such a policy, I don't know one reporter or commentator who wouldn't enjoy being an informer or a stool pigeon.

I can see the day when the news media would serve two masters with pride, as well as efficiency.

"Hello, Jordan, Kelly here. There's been a bank robbery at Fifth and Maple. Three masked men got away with five hundred thousand dollars."

"Great, Kelly, give me the facts."

"I don't have them."

"What do you mean you don't have them?"

"The cops subpoenaed my notebook."

"Well, just tell me what happened."

"I can't. The FBI said I couldn't talk about the case."

"Look, Kelly, I didn't send you out to cover a story so you'd keep your mouth shut. This is news."

"I told that to the deputy attorney general, but he said when three people are kidnapped in a bank robbery, my first obligation is to the courts."

"Three people were kidnapped?"

"I wasn't supposed to tell you that. If you print it, I'll be held in contempt."

"Good grief, Kelly, your loyalties are to the paper. What happened?"

"It's no good, Jordan. Even if I told you the bank manager's wife's boyfriend is believed to have engineered the robbery, I'd be in Dutch."

"The boyfriend of the bank manager's wife?"

"Yah. Jerry got a great photo of him coming out of the bank, with the money in one hand and the wife of the bank manager on his other arm. They escaped on top of a Greyhound bus."

"Jerry got a picture of that?"

"A sequence of pictures."

"Where are the photos?"

"The cops took them as evidence. They also arrested Jerry for being at the scene of a crime. I would have gone to his aid, but I heard over the police radio that the Greyhound bus had been stopped at a roadblock, so I rushed over there just as the cops were climbing on the bus to make the arrests."

"They got the people who heisted the bank?"

"Can't tell you that."

"Kelly, please, Kelly. We go to press in an hour. Were they arrested?"

"I'm not at liberty to divulge any facts, other than to say that the explosions I heard going on for over an hour did not come from the exhaust pipe of the bus."

"For God's sake, Kelly, give me anything—the name of the bank—anything."

"I'm sorry, Jordan, I probably should not even have called in."

"Where the devil are you?"

"Down here at the Justice Department. They let me make one phone call."

"Have you been arrested, too?"

"Not exactly, but the Justice Department said that without influencing what I wrote, they were holding me as a material witness until the final edition of our paper hits the stand."

"I'll get you out, Kelly."

"I might as well stay here. I have to testify in the Morgan hijacking case that I covered for you last week."

FIRST THE BIBLE,
THEN SHAKESPEARE

Now that the best minds in the Western world have "improved" the Bible in the most modern edition, which is called the New English Bible (the new Twenty-third Psalm begins, "The Lord is my shepherd, I shall want nothing. He makes me lie down in green pastures and leads me beside the waters of peace; He renews life within me and for His name's sake guides me in the right path. . . ."), it has been decided to update Shakespeare and make him easier for people to understand.

With this goal in mind and using the New English Bible as our inspiration, a group of us has already managed to update some of Hamlet's soliloquy.

"To be or not to be" will soon read as follows:

Should I or shouldn't I? That is the question.
I don't know whether it would be better for me to
Take
A lot of guff and that sort of thing
Or to fight back against all this trouble I've been
Having.
Maybe I should drop dead, and sleep;
That's all. And by sleeping hope to end
All this emotional conflict
That everyone goes through; boy, wouldn't that be a
Solution?
If you could just cop out, close your eyes and
Sleep. And maybe have a few good dreams. But that's
The trouble.
If you're dead, who knows what kind of bad trips
You're going to have
Leaving the station? It sure gives you something to
Think about.
You have to show some respect; if you don't, you
Could be in for real trouble.

That's as far as we got with Hamlet. But we have also been working on *Romeo and Juliet*.

So far, it goes like this:

JULIET (*on balcony to herself*): O Romeo, Romeo. Why are you Romeo? Why don't you change your name? Or if you can't do it, I'll work it out some way so I won't be known as a Capulet.

ROMEO (*underneath balcony to himself*): I wonder if I should stick around and listen to what she's saying, or speak up and jawbone with her.

JULIET: The only thing I hold against you, Romeo, is your name. Personally I like you for yourself, and not because you're a Montague.

Like, what's a Montague? It isn't your hand or your foot or your face, or any other part of your body belonging to a man. Gosh, I wish you had another name.

But what's in a name? Suppose you saw this flower which was called something else besides a rose. It would still smell pretty good, wouldn't it?

And that's the way it is with Romeo. If his name, for example, were Irving, he still would be perfect in my book. Romeo, get rid of your name because it has nothing to do with you, and in exchange, I'll do anything you want me to.

ROMEO (*out loud*): OK, Juliet, it's a deal. Forget I'm Romeo and call me Loverboy instead.

JULIET: Who is that listening in on everything I've been saying?

ROMEO: I can't tell you who I am because I hate my name, and from what I can tell, you do, too.

JULIET: Unless I'm stone-deaf, you sound like Romeo Montague. Are you or aren't you?

ROMEO: It all depends if it shakes you up or not.

As you see, we still have a little work to do, but if it took twenty years to rewrite the Bible, I believe we've gotten off to a pretty good start.

CIVIL DEFENSE AND TELEVISION

The recent fiasco at NORAD, when the wrong tape was inserted in a computer, warning the country that there was a national emergency and all TV and radio stations should go off the air, boggles the imagination.

The message containing code words "hatefulness, hatefulness" was supposed to be used only for a real nuclear attack. The fact that the message was ignored by most TV and radio stations shows how serious the credibility gap is in this country between the people and its government.

Civil defense and military leaders are now investigating the foul-up and trying to find new fail-safe methods of alerting the public to a nuclear missile attack.

My friend Wafferman was explaining at dinner the other night what had happened at NORAD, when his seventeen-year-old son, Joel, raised some disturbing questions.

"Why would they want to turn off all the television programs and radio shows in case of a nuclear attack?"

"Because," Wafferman said, "it would give President Nixon an opportunity to go on the air and calm the people."

"I don't want to hear President Nixon just before I die," Joel said adamantly.

"You're not going to die," Wafferman said. "The reason for the alert is to allow everyone to prepare himself for a nuclear attack."

"I read somewhere that we will only have a half hour before we get zonked."

"That's about right," Wafferman replied.

"Well, what are we supposed to do in that half hour?"

"I don't know," Wafferman said, getting slightly irritated. "That's what President Nixon is supposed to tell us when all the TV stations go off the air."

"Maybe we're supposed to fill our bathtubs with water?" Joel said.

"I don't like you being sarcastic about nuclear war. It's very unpatriotic."

"Or maybe he'll tell us to run outside and put plastic over our heads."

"It's typical of your generation," Wafferman said, trying not to lose his temper, "that even when there is a nuclear attack, you have no faith in the President of the United States."

"I do have faith in the President. He'll probably describe it as the greatest nuclear attack in the history of mankind. But if I have a half hour to live, I'd rather watch *I Love Lucy*."

"Now let me tell you something. This civilian warning system has been worked out by the best brains in this country," Wafferman said. "Millions and millions of dollars have been spent to give every man, woman, and child in this country thirty minutes' notice before the enemy strikes. Without the warning system, none of us would ever know what hit us."

"I'd even settle for a rerun of *McHale's Navy*," Joel said.

"I don't see any reason to continue this discussion," Wafferman said, "if you can't see the importance of civil defense in time of nuclear attack."

"I see the importance of it," Joel replied. "But what I don't understand is why we can't watch a good television show just before we go. Why can't a compromise be worked out? Nixon can be on one of the channels, and the other stations can continue their regular programming. Then people will at least have a choice of what they can watch in the last thirty minutes of their lives."

Joel started to laugh.

"What's so funny?" Wafferman asked.

"I'd like to be around, just to see the TV ratings the next day."

THE INVENTION OF TV

The question came up at dinner the other night when people were discussing the Tory victory in Great Britain.

"Why is it that the English were able to rule the world for almost two hundred years, while the United States has been unable to hold on for less than twenty-five years?"

An Englishman at the table replied, "It's quite simple, my dear chap. There was no television."

"Of course," someone else said, "television hadn't been invented then!"

"On the contrary," the Englishman said, "it had been invented, but we were wise enough not to let the secret out."

We all looked at him in amazement.

"Lord Cashmere of Rutland invented television in the year 1775," he said. "You can look it up in the secret archives of the British Museum. He was actually trying to invent the radio; rather than sound, he got a picture on his box instead."

"What kind of a picture?" a skeptical guest asked.

"A picture of a Redcoat in Boston flogging a Colonial old man."

"It is hard to believe," someone said.

"Quite. In any case, Lord Cashmere knew he was onto something big, so he took the box to King George III and demonstrated it to the court, which at the time was meeting on the Television Moors in Wales."

"So that's where the name came from," someone said.

"It's all in the secret archives," the Englishman said. "The court was aghast at what they were seeing. There were large, burly Redcoats beating on the poor Colonials, kicking women and children, setting fire to their homes, and committing unbelievable atrocities in the villages.

" 'Lord Cashmere,' the Archbishop of Canterbury said, 'what in God's name have you wrought?'

"Lord Cashmere said, 'I'm not sure, but it's possible that this invention could change all of mankind. Just think, my noble friends, that with this box our people would bear witness to the great news events of our time. No longer would we be dependent on ships for our news. We could actually see our victories as they were happening. What a boost for the morale of the empire.'

"A cheer rent the air over Television Moors. But then General Sir Ronald Paley, the king's adviser on military affairs, spoke up: 'I do not wish to dash cold water on this box, but may I point out to you gentlemen that this invention could be the end of the empire? Do you believe our young people would remain silent after watching what we were doing in the Colonies, or, for that matter, anywhere else? The country would be split asunder. The strength of England is that her people have no idea of what we're up to abroad.'

"King George III spoke up. 'Sir Ronald is right. If we're to wage war in the Colonies, we don't want the people at home to know what we're doing.

" 'Besides, if we have to pull out, I want to do it without the whole world watching us. Lord Cashmere, you have done your country an ill deed by this damnable contraption. I order you at the pain of losing your head never to reveal your secret. We shall bury the box here on the moors, and Britannia will rule the waves.' "

The Englishman paused as we hung onto his every word.

"Then you kept the secret all these years," someone said.

"That's correct," the Englishman said. "Thirty years ago an American anthropologist, digging around the moors, discovered the box. He turned it over to RCA who, without thinking of the consequences, started to manufacture them on a large scale. I imagine you can date the difficulty of the United States as a world power from the day Lord Cashmere's box was made available to the world."

"What a great story," I said. "Do you mind if I write it?"

"Go right ahead," the Englishman said. "It can't do Britain any harm anymore."

ROOTING FOR WALTER

We had another space-shot success recently, and while I still get excited about these things, I notice that every time we have a splashdown, more and more people look at me as if to say "What else is new?" I discovered this is particularly true of people under twenty-one years of age.

During the recent Apollo flights, I found my wife and myself spending more and more time alone in front of the TV set while our children were sulking somewhere in the house because their favorite TV show had been preempted.

"Come down and see pictures of the moon," I would yell, only to hear someone upstairs yell back, "We've ALREADY seen pictures of the moon."

"But these are in color."

"There's nothing to see but rocks."

"But they're not even on this planet," I would yell back up.

A voice would come back bitterly, "They shouldn't have taken *Lucy* off the air."

All the networks do a good job on these space shots. I like Jules Bergman of ABC, and I'm always indebted to Frank McGee for his chalk talks on what is going on there in outer space. But, without disparaging the job these fine men do, my wife and I seem to identify more with Walter Cronkite.

My wife identifies with Cronkite even more than she does with the astronauts.

If Walter's relaxed, she's relaxed; if Walter gets nervous, my wife gets nervous. Walter Cronkite, more than anyone else, sees us through these shots, and we really count on him to get the Apollo capsules back safely to earth.

I remember the night of all the trouble. My wife and I were sitting there drinking coffee. Walter had told us how well the lunar module, named Snoopy, had behaved on its first pass at the moon. He said it had been perfect, except

52

for some camera trouble, which we could hardly blame Walter for.

Now Snoopy was on its second pass at the moon. After jettisoning its descent stage engine, it started up its 3,500-pound thrust engine which was supposed to get it back to the mother Apollo ship, Charlie Brown.

Suddenly something went wrong, and we heard Cernan's voice say "Son of a bitch." Walter, who up to that time was calmly telling us what was happening, became serious.

My wife jumped up from the chair. "What is it, Walter?" she cried. "What's happening?"

"Sit down," I said to her. "Don't panic. Walter will inform us."

"I can tell he's scared," she said.

Walter told us Snoopy was barreling, apparently out of control. In the background we could hear Cernan cursing as he and Stafford, according to Walter, were trying to get Snoopy under control.

"Why doesn't Walter do something?" my wife said.

"He's not in charge of the mission," I told her. "All he's doing is reporting what's happening."

"Well, he's the only one I have faith in," she said. "What do the rest of them know?"

By this time the crisis seemed to have passed and Snoopy had managed to get out of its roll. Walter looked relieved, but at the same time he informed us that something of such a serious nature might mean the postponement of Apollo 11 and the moon landing.

"Walter's going to scrub the moon shot," my wife said.

"He's not going to scrub it," I said, "but he wants to know exactly what happened before he gives the OK on Apollo eleven. You can't blame him."

A few minutes later, Walter, looking much less tense, came back to tell us that the trouble had been a switch that didn't turn on. He said that although it gave him a fright, the moon shot would take place in July.

My wife sighed. "I knew Walter wouldn't let us down."

THE SHOCK OF RECOGNITION

Recently, New York City had a blackout which caused all nine television stations in the area to go out for several hours. This created tremendous crisis in families all over the New York area and proved that TV plays a much greater role in people's lives than anyone can imagine.

For example, when the TV set went off in the Bufkins' house in Forest Hills, panic set in. First, Bufkins thought it was his set in the living room, so he rushed into his bedroom and turned on that set. Nothing.

The phone rang and Mrs. Bufkins heard her sister in Manhattan tell her that there was a blackout.

She hung up and said to her husband, "It isn't your set. Something's happened to the top of the Empire State Building."

Bufkins stopped and said, "Who are you?"

"I'm your wife, Edith."

"Oh," Bufkins said. "Then I suppose those kids in there are mine."

"That's right," Mrs. Bufkins said. "If you ever got out of that armchair in front of the TV set, you'd know who we were."

"Boy, they've really grown," Bufkins said, looking at his son and daughter. "How old are they now?"

"Thirteen and fourteen," Mrs. Bufkins replied.

"I'll be darned. Hi, kids."

"Who's he?" Bufkins' son, Henry, asked.

"It's your father," Mrs. Bufkins said.

"I'm pleased to meetcha," Bufkins' daughter, Mary, said shyly.

There was an embarrassed silence all around.

"Look," said Bufkins finally. "I know I haven't been much of a father, but now that the TV's out, I'd like to make it up to you."

"How?" asked Henry.

"Well, let's just talk," Bufkins said. "That's the best way to get to know each other."

"What do you want to talk about?" Mary asked.

"Well, for starters, what school do you go to?"

"We go to Forest Hills HS," Henry said.

"What do you know?" Bufkins said. "You're both in high school."

There was dead silence.

"What do *you* do?" Mary asked.

"I'm an accountant," Bufkins said.

"I thought you were a car salesman," Mrs. Bufkins said in surprise.

"That was two years ago. Didn't I tell you I changed jobs?" Bufkins said in surprise.

"No, you didn't. You haven't told me anything for two years."

"Yup. I'm doing quite well too," Bufkins said.

"Then why am I working in a department store?" Mrs. Bufkins demanded.

"Oh, are you still working in a department store? If I had known that, I would have told you you could quit last year. You should have mentioned it," Bufkins said.

There was more dead silence.

Finally Henry said, "Hey, you want to hear me play the guitar?"

"I'll be darned. You know how to play the guitar? Say, didn't I have a daughter who played the guitar?"

"That was Susie," Mrs. Bufkins said.

"Where is she?"

"She got married a year ago, just about the time you were watching the World Series."

"How about that?" Bufkins said, very pleased. "You know, I hope they don't fix the antenna for another couple of hours. There's nothing like a blackout for a man to *really* get to know his family."

3

THE NAKED MAN

THE MOON IS DOWN

The trouble with scientists is that they can't leave well enough alone. They were able to get a man to the moon and that was a good thing. They had man bring back rocks from the moon to examine, and that was certainly a noble endeavor. Then someone thought up the idea of having a lunar module crash into the moon to see how much the moon would quake, and while that was sort of messy, it was something most people went along with.

But apparently it was just the beginning. At a meeting in Los Angeles a scientist named Gary Latham proposed that we fire off an atomic bomb on the dark side of the moon to find out what the core is made of.

I am certain that if this idea is finally agreed to, our scientists will not be satisfied to stop there. I predict that if we go ahead with an explosion on the moon, this will eventually happen:

"Gentlemen, as you are all aware, our atomic explosion on the moon was tremendously successful. We now know the core of the moon is composed of hard rubber, similar to that used in a golf ball. The question today is: What do we do to the moon next?"

"Professor, my department has been making studies, and we believe it is feasible to knock off a large section of the moon with an intercontinental ballastic missile and then, with a giant magnet, which we would build in Nevada, attract the piece of moon to earth. Thus we would be able to study the moon in an earth environment and not be dependent on a bagful of rocks for our information."

"In all due respect, Professor Heitel, my department has come up with an idea far superior to yours. We feel that with the right conditions we can put the moon on a collision course with another planet and register the impact at the moment it collides. This will give us invaluable information on how other planets react when hit by a large body of dead mass."

"That's not good enough, Professor Runkle. The most important thing to be learned is what would happen if the moon was removed from the earth's orbit. Until we know this, we cannot continue our future experiments. At the moment, the moon is too large to be pushed out of orbit. But if we broke it up into little pieces, by firing a series of hydrogen bombs in a volley for three days, we could smash the moon to bits. The small pieces could then be pushed out of orbit by our spaceships and we could track their paths."

"I do not object to the idea, Professor Grimsted, except that we don't want to contaminate other planets, just in case there is life on them. My people feel that if there was some way we could set fire to the moon, we could photograph it in color while it was burning up, which then could give us clues to the unanswered questions we still have about the sun."

"Gentlemen, gentlemen. All your ideas have merit.

"We seem to be agreed that the moon is expendable. The only question is how best to destroy it and still get the most scientific data. Our laboratories in Carlsbad may have a solution. They have perfected a powerful chemical which, when fired by an SBM-4 rocket, could turn the moon into a thick muddy soup which would drip down on the earth.

"If our calculations are correct, the major part of the soup would drip down off the beaches at Santa Barbara, California, giving us valuable information as to what happens when the moon's surface is blended with crude oil."

WHITE RATS HAVE ALL THE FUN

The key to man's survival on earth seems to be the white rat. Most experiments being conducted these days to see what effect our environment has on human beings are first conducted on white rats. Only after we know what happens to white rats will we take any action to protect the human race.

Nobody has bothered to find out how the rats feel about this. In man's ever-questing search for truth, I visited a large government laboratory the other evening around midnight and recorded what the white rats were saying to each other.

"Zelda, you look so thin."

"They've had me on cyclamates. I must have lost three ounces in a week. What have you been doing?"

"I've been taking monosodium glutamate. It's tasty, but it gives me headaches. Oh, Horace, will you stop coughing?"

"Ack, ack, ack. I can't help it. They've got me smoking a pack of cigarettes a day."

"Why don't you give them up?"

"I'd like to, but they won't let me."

"What on earth is Sheldon doing? He's staggering all over his cage."

"He's involved in the marijuana experiments. He goes on a trip every night."

"That's what I call luck. How can I get off cyclamates and in the pot program?"

"You have to know somebody. Every rat in the lab wants to go on pot."

"I don't. I feel you have to face reality and not seek escape. That's why I'm proud to be associated with the air pollution project."

"How can you stand it?"

"It's not bad. Every day they drive me around New York City and I just breathe. If I die, they know the air pollution count is too high. If I live, I get to see the city."

"You're probably right, Bettina. I volunteered for air pollution, but some computer assigned me to water pollution. I'm getting sick of drinking dirty river water every day."

"What's the matter with Whitney? He seems awfully quiet tonight."

"He's been eating grapes with DDT on them for a week, and I guess it's finally getting to him."

"I told him to boycott grapes."

"They won't give him anything else to eat, so he has no choice."

"Where's Alvin?"

"Didn't you hear? They transplanted his heart today into Hazel. Hers gave out during the automobile exhaust tests."

"Poor Alvin."

"He didn't seem to mind. He was involved in the tranquilizer experiments, and when they asked him for his heart, he said he couldn't care less."

"Who's crying?"

"Sandra. They have her taking the birth control pill. She wants babies in the worst way."

"Well, at least she's having some fun, which is more than I can say for what I'm doing."

"What's that, Carlton?"

"I'm working for NASA to see the effects of weightlessness. I vomit all the time."

"But the space program at least has some glamor to it. They keep injecting me with flu germs."

"I guess Sampson has the best job of any of us."

"What is he doing?"

"They put him in front of a color television set all day long to see how much radiation he absorbs. He's the only white rat I know who gets to watch *Laugh-In*."

WHICH SIDE ARE YOU ON?

Sometimes one gets the feeling that the right-hand germs in the government don't know what the left-hand germs are doing. This was brought home to me the other day when I read about the millions of dollars that were being spent to see that the astronauts did not bring back a single germ from the moon.

Unfortunately, across the page from that story was another that the Army was going ahead with open-air testing of nerve gases and germ warfare.

I was sure it was a mistake, so I went to see my friend

Professor Heinrich Applebaum, the government micro-biologist and germ warfare expert.

"Professor, I don't understand why we're going to so much trouble protecting the earth from moon germs when we are still experimenting with germs for warfare."

"One does not have anything to do with the other," Applebaum said angrily. "We must be certain in our space program that we do not do anything to contaminate the earth. This is essential to the survival of mankind."

"Then why are we experimenting on earth with germs for war?"

"Ah, that's different. If we contaminate the earth with germs, everyone understands that we are only defending ourselves from the other side. But if we brought back moon germs and something happened, no one would forgive us."

"What kinds of germs could be on the moon that are any worse than the germs you're experimenting with right now?"

Applebaum said, "We don't know what kind of germs they have on the moon, and we have to be particularly cautious to make sure our astronauts don't bring back infection. After all, the space program is devoted to peace. Now, the germs we have here we know about, and those germs are important to our defense program."

"But what if you had an accident in which the earth germs got out of the laboratories or escaped from the testing area?"

"We don't like to think about things like that. If we did, we wouldn't have a germ warfare program."

"But how can the same people on one hand spend all this money to see that no germs come back from the moon, and on the other spend money to figure out ways of spreading germs around the world?"

"You don't understand," said Applebaum, slamming his fist on the desk. "It's two different departments. The Defense Department doesn't tell NASA what to do with their germs, and NASA doesn't tell the Defense Department what to do with their germs."

"Well," I said, "why doesn't the Defense Department

do its germ testing on the moon? In that way there would be less danger of contaminating the earth."

"Because," said Applebaum, breaking a test tube in his hand, "we don't want to contaminate the moon. We know the earth is contaminated, but we're hoping to keep the moon clean."

"For what reason?"

"Because someday we may want to test earth germs in a germless atmosphere."

"I have one thought, Professor. They wouldn't let President Nixon have dinner with the three astronauts because the doctors were afraid his germs might affect them. Why don't they make it up to the President by letting him have dinner with the people in the Defense Department who are working on germ warfare?"

Applebaum screamed at me, "Get out of here. And don't come back."

THE NAKED MAN

A new book will soon appear on the market which will cause a sensation in scientific circles. It is titled *The Naked Man* and it was written by Frederick III, a chimpanzee attached to the Rockefeller Institute. Frederick III was involved in some enzyme experiments at the institute which took up only a few hours of his day. Because he was restless, the directors gave him a typewriter to play with. You can imagine their surprise when, instead of just messing around, Frederick wrote a book.

Frederick's book—and this is the shocker—claims that all chimpanzees, monkeys and apes evolved from man. He says that man was the first primate before there were apes of any kind.

Frederick is not certain when man first appeared on earth, though he suspects it was at least 30,000,000 years ago. As time went on and man went through many stages, he started to develop many apelike qualities until today it is easy for apes to identify with man and realize how much they have in common.

Many apes and chimpanzees are horrified to think they resemble man in any way, and a chimpanzee named Treetop, with the National Institute of Mental Health, has written a paper denouncing Frederick III's thesis. Treetop maintains that although in some respects men are looking more and more like apes, the ape could not have possibly evolved from man. He has attacked Frederick III's research on the grounds that, except for the few men he has come into contact with at the Rockefeller Institute, the only other men he has observed are flower children in the park that he can see from his caged window.

Frederick says in his book that the similarities between apes and man are greater than one might think. Man today is behaving as apes used to behave before they were civilized. Man puts great emphasis on territory and seems to be willing to kill to protect his turf. As a lower form of ape, man is unable to deal with any situation without screaming and shouting. Frederick cites examples where men have been placed in large apartment buildings for lengths of time and have gone berserk.

Treetop says that man's behavior is more similar to rats than to apes, and while man behaves irrationally in almost any situation and may resort to extreme measures when endangered, it does not follow that just because men beat their chests and growl, they belong to the ape family.

Frederick thinks that the primitive personality traits of man have been adapted by apes. Having studied man under laboratory conditions, Frederick has discovered that the eating habits and sex life of *Homo sapiens* follow a pattern similar to those practiced by modern apes. Survival seems to be the basic principle in man's jungle, and while apes do not resort to violence unless provoked, man has not yet evolved to a point in his development where he can tell why he behaves the way he does.

Treetop disagrees. He maintains that man has gone as far as he'll ever go and hasn't changed from the day he was born. The instinct in men to destroy is so strong that it is slander to class them in any way with apes.

Frederick's response to that is to cite King Kong's

destruction of the Empire State Building as something man might do.

Treetop says King Kong was an exception to the rule, and it's unfair to use one gorilla's behavior as a sample.

In any case, when the book comes out, there will be a continuing controversy on it. On one side will be the apes who will hate to acknowledge they have inherited any characteristics from man. On the other side will be those monkeys, chimpanzees and gorillas who will admit that some of their traits are possibly man-evolved and will now try to deal with the problem in an apelike way.

THE IMPOSSIBLE DREAM

I was in New York the other day and took a ride with a friend of mine in a taxi. When we got out of the cab, my friend said to the driver, "Thank you for the ride. You did a superb job of driving."

The taxi driver was stunned for a second. Then he said, "Are you a wise guy or something?"

"No, my dear man, and I'm not putting you on. I admire the way you keep your cool in heavy traffic."

"Yeh," the driver said and drove off.

"What was that all about?" I asked.

"I am trying to bring love back to New York," he said. "I believe it's the only thing that can save the city."

"How can one man save New York?"

"It's not one man. I believe I have made that taxi driver's day. Suppose he has twenty fares. He's going to be nice to those twenty fares because someone was nice to him. Those fares in turn will be kinder to their employees or shopkeepers or waiters or even their own families. They, in turn, will be nicer to other people. Eventually the goodwill could spread to at least a thousand people. Now that isn't bad, is it?"

"But you're depending on that taxi driver to pass your goodwill to others."

"I'm not depending on it," my friend said. "I'm aware that the system isn't foolproof. I might deal with ten different people today. If, out of ten, I can make three happy, then eventually I can indirectly influence the attitudes of three thousand more."

"It sounds good on paper," I admitted, "but I'm not sure it works in practice."

"Nothing is lost if it doesn't. It didn't take any of my time to tell that man he was doing a good job. He neither received a larger tip nor a smaller tip. If it fell on deaf ears, so what? Tomorrow there will be another taxi driver whom I can try to make happy."

"You're some kind of a nut," I said.

"That shows you how cynical you have become. I have made a study of this. The thing that seems to be lacking, besides money of course, for our postal employees is that no one tells people who work for the post office what a good job they're doing."

"But they're not doing a good job."

"They're not doing a good job because they feel no one cares if they do or not. Why shouldn't someone say a kind word to them?"

We were walking past a structure in the process of being built and passed five workmen eating their lunch. My friend stopped. "That's a magnificent job you men have done. It must be difficult and dangerous work."

The five men eyed my friend suspiciously.

"When will it be finished?"

"June," a man grunted.

"Ah! That really is impressive. You must all be very proud."

We walked away. I said to him, "I haven't seen anyone like you since *The Man of La Mancha*."

"When those men digest my words, they will feel better for it. Somehow the city will benefit from their happiness."

"But you can't do this all alone!" I protested. "You're just one man."

"The most important thing is not to get discouraged. Making people in the city become kind again is not an easy job, but if I can enlist other people in my campaign. . . ."

"You just winked at a very plain-looking woman," I said.

"Yes, I know," he replied. "And if she's a school-teacher, her class will be in for a fantastic day."

4

TROUBLE IN PARADISE

THE CLEANEST SHIRTS IN TOWN

Everyone talks about water pollution, but no one seems to know who started it. The history of modern water pollution in the United States dates back to February 28, 1931, when Mrs. Frieda Murphy leaned over her back-yard fence and said to Mrs. Sophie Holbrook, "You call those shirts white?"

Mrs. Holbrook blushed and said, "They're as white as I can get them with this ordinary laundry soap."

"What you should use is this Formula Cake soap which guarantees against the dull-washtub-gray look that the family wash has always had."

Skeptical but adventurous, Mrs. Holbrook tried the Formula Cake soap, which happily did take the gray out of her husband's shirts. But what Mrs. Holbrook didn't know was that after the water was drained from the tub, it emptied into the sewer, which emptied into the Blue Sky River, killing two fish.

Three years later Mrs. Murphy leaned over the fence and said to Mrs. Holbrook, "It's none of my business, but are you still using that Formula Cake soap?"

"Yes, I am."

"No wonder your husband's shirts always look dirty around the collar."

"I can never get the dirt off the collar," Mrs. Holbrook cried.

"You can if you use Klonk Soap Chips. They were designed especially for collar dirt. Here, you can have my box."

Mrs. Holbrook used the Klonk, and the next time her husband put on his shirt, he remarked, "How on earth did you get the collar clean?"

"That's my secret," said Mrs. Holbrook, and then she whispered to no one in particular, "and Mrs. Murphy's."

But, unbeknownst to Mrs. Holbrook, the water from Klonk Soap Chips prevented any fish downstream from hatching eggs.

Four years later, Mrs. Murphy was hanging up her shirts and Mrs. Holbrook said, "How did you ever get your cuffs so white, surely not with Klonk?"

"Not ordinary Klonk," Mrs. Murphy said. "But I did with Super Fortified Klonk with the XLP additive. You see, Super Fortified Klonk attacks dirt and destroys it. Here, try it on your shirts."

Mrs. Holbrook did and discovered her husband's shirt cuffs turned pure white. What she couldn't possibly know was that it turned the river water pure white as well.

The years went by, and poor Mrs. Murphy died. Her daughter-in-law took over the house. Mrs. Holbrook noticed how the daughter-in-law used to always sing as she hung up her wash.

"Why do you always sing?" asked Mrs. Holbrook.

"Because of this New Dynamite detergent. It literally dynamites my clothes clean. Here, try it, and then let's go to a movie, since Dynamite detergent takes the drudgery out of washing."

Six months later the Blue Sky River was declared a health hazard.

Finally, last year Mrs. Murphy's daughter-in-law called over to Mrs. Holbrook, "Have you heard about Zap, the enzyme giant killer?"

A few days later, as Mr. Holbrook was walking home from work, he accidentally fell into the Blue Sky River, swallowed a mouthful of water, and died immediately.

At the funeral services the minister said, "You can say anything you want about Holbrook, but no one can deny he had the cleanest shirts in town."

WHAT TAHITIANS THINK

There have been two explosions in the South Pacific recently. One is the French atomic bomb, and the other is the tourist invasion of Polynesia. It is predicted that while the fallout from the former will blow away, the fallout from the tourist explosion will be around for centuries to come.

Tahiti and the other islands in the South Pacific are caught between cultures. The airplane has made it possible to fly to Tahiti in a matter of hours. The only ones who aren't awed by this are the Tahitians. They don't know who designed the 707 jet, but they'd just as soon he'd drown in the nearest atoll.

For hundreds and hundreds of years Tahitians have set their own pace, which is somewhat slower than that of Americans and Europeans.

In order to enjoy the islands, you must understand the thinking of the Tahitians.

The American says, "Please, I must have breakfast immediately because I have to catch a plane for Pago Pago."

"Yes, sir," the Tahitian says. But he thinks, "I have already had breakfast, and, besides, I do not have a plane to catch, so why is he bothering me with his problem?"

Ten minutes later the American says, "Waiter, I must have breakfast now!"

"Yes, sir," the Tahitian says. But he thinks to himself, "If I do not give him his breakfast, perhaps the French manager will fire me and then I can go fishing in the lagoon."

Fifteen minutes later a fuming American says, "See here, I have been waiting for breakfast for twenty-five minutes. I haven't even had coffee. I have five countries to see in six days. When I get back to the United States, I will tell all my friends not to come to Tahiti."

"Yes, sir," the Tahitian says, wiping the counter. But he thinks, "If he would only keep his promise, then this hotel would close, and I could sleep with my papaya all day long."

The tourist says sternly, "Your economy depends on tourism, and you will never prosper and become rich if you don't learn that tourists like to be served fast."

"I know." The Tahitian nods sadly. But he thinks to himself, "Who wants to become rich if it makes you so nervous?"

"Don't get me wrong," the tourist says. "I admire your life-style. But one must get with the twentieth century. You can't just dillydally all day long. You have to go, go, go."

"Thank you," the Tahitian says. But he thinks, "I wouldn't have to put up with all this garbage if I had gone canoeing with Fredo this morning."

A half hour later the American is now steaming and shouting for the French manager, who is also steaming and yelling.

The Tahitian smiles at both of them and thinks to himself sadly, "I would hate to be a tourist in Tahiti because it's almost impossible to get anything to eat."

MOTHER NATURE'S LAST WILL

The other night I was home reading a book when I received a telephone call that Mother Nature was dying. I dressed hurriedly and rushed over to the hospital. A lot of people had gotten there before me, and they were all sitting in the waiting room crying and wringing their hands. I searched out the doctors who were in another room having a heated argument as to how to save her. Each doctor seemed to have a different remedy:

One doctor said, "We have to get her some fresh air. She can't breathe. We'll have to turn off the power plant because of the smoke."

"Are you out of your mind?" another doctor said. "We turn off the power, and she'll freeze to death."

"Perhaps we could keep all cars away from the hospital," a third doctor suggested. "That would relieve her breathing."

"Out of the question," a fourth doctor barked. "How would we get back and forth to work if we prohibited cars near the hospital?"

"Gentlemen," another doctor said, "I don't believe it's the air that is hurting her as much as the water. We have to find some water that's drinkable. Strong measures must be taken immediately against polluting the hospital water."

The director said, "Where would we get the money to support the hospital if we closed down the factories because they're polluting the streams?"

"We'd also have to give up detergents," a doctor added, "and we can't have a clean hospital if you give up detergents."

"Isn't anybody going to do anything?" I shouted.

They saw me for the first time, and one of the doctors said angrily, "We're sorry, this is a medical conference for professionals only. Would you kindly leave?"

I walked out and down the hall. Suddenly I saw a closed room, which had the name MOTHER NATURE hand-printed on the door. Underneath it, in large red letters, was another sign: NO VISITORS.

No one was in the hall, so I opened the door. There was Mother Nature propped up on pillows. She looked old and tired and haggard. I couldn't believe anyone could have changed so much in ten short years. But she seemed glad to see someone and smiled weakly.

"Hi, Ma," I said. "You're looking swell."

"You wouldn't kid a very sick lady, would you?" she said, gasping.

"No, I'm not kidding. You look wonderful.

"I've just been talking to the doctors, and they say they'll have you on your feet in no time."

"Those quacks don't know anything," she said. "All they do is come in every few hours and take my temperature and give me something to relieve the pain. I think I've had it this time."

"Don't talk that way, Ma. You're going to pull through. You've survived worse things than this before."

"It's never been this bad," she said and then started having a coughing fit. "This time the Grim Reaper's coming to get me."

"But if you go, we'll all have to go, Ma," I cried. "You have to hold on. Please, Ma."

"I kept complaining of pain," she whispered, "but no one would pay attention to me. I said, 'If you keep doing what you're doing, I'm going to die.' But everyone said, 'Ma, you'll never die.' Why didn't they listen to me?"

"We're listening now, Ma. We're listening. We have the best doctors in the world. They're out there now, and they have a plan."

"I guess the real thing that hurts," she said, "is that my will won't be worth anything now. I left every person in the world clear water, pure air, green fields, brilliant sunsets and blue skies. It wasn't much, but it was everything I had."

Just then the door opened and a nurse came in. She went over to the bed waving a thermometer.

"Come on, Mother. It's time to take your temperature."

"NOT ONE RUBLE"

A top-secret meeting of Kremlin officials was held last week to discuss the latest defense strategy against the United States. Comrade Alexander Potomski, in charge of the Third Bureau in the United States, was the first to make his report.

"Comrades, I am happy to report that air pollution in the United States has risen more than one hundred and forty million tons, which is ten million tons more than last year."

There was applause from everyone in the room.

"How did you manage this, Comrade Potomski?" one of the members of the Presidium asked.

"I wish I could take the credit, but the Americans have done it themselves. At the present rate of air pollution everyone in the United States should be dead in twenty years."

"But surely," a marshal said, "the Americans must be aware of what air pollution is doing to them."

"They are, but it doesn't matter. They have many pressure groups who scream that if something serious were done about air pollution, it would hurt their businesses. So the government leaders talk about the problem and do nothing."

"Then we can count on air pollution in the United States for the foreseeable future?"

"I cannot see the Americans doing anything serious about it for a long time to come," said Comrade Potomski.

Comrade Redhevnov of the Fifth Bureau got up. "Comrades, I also have good news. The Americans are polluting their water at such a rate that in ten years they will make every river, stream and lake undrinkable, unswimmable and uninhabitable for fish."

There was more applause from everyone in the room.

"Why are we spending money to pollute American waters?" the First Secretary of the Communist Party of Leningrad asked. "If the Americans found out, they could take serious action against us."

"We are not doing it," Comrade Redhevnov said. "The Americans are doing it to themselves."

There were cries of derision.

The Chairman of the Presidium asked, "Are you trying to tell us that the Americans are poisoning their own water?"

"Exactly, Comrade Chairman. They pour sewage into it. Factories spew out every kind of chemical and detergent and put anything you can think of in the water supply."

"But surely the Americans are not stupid people. If they knew they were poisoning their own water, they would demand a stop to it."

Comrade Redhevnov said, "I know it's hard to believe, comrades, but even though they know what they're doing, they still keep doing it. If they stopped pollution, the polluters say, they would stop production of goods the Americans need. So no one is going to give the polluters any serious trouble."

"Excellent," said the Kremlin planners. "So far, it hasn't cost us a ruble."

Comrade Sokolov of the Sixth Bureau, charged with studying American transportation, got up to make his report. "I have the best news, comrades. The American transportation system is breaking down. The railroads are shot, the roads are impassable, and the airports are so congested that flying is nearly hopeless.

"In five years the crisis will have reached a point where nothing in the United States can move."

Once again there were cheers.

"Comrade Sokolov, you have accomplished the impossible dream."

"Comrades, the Americans have done it all by themselves. They are so intent on selling cars, moving freight, and booking airplane seats that they refuse to face what they're doing to the country."

There were murmurs all around the conference table. Finally the chairman said, "From what you have told us, there doesn't seem to be any sense in the Soviet Union spending vast sums of money for new weapons against the United States.

"Therefore, I make the following recommendation."

Everyone held his breath.

The chairman said, "We all sit tight."

SCHOOL FOR LUGGAGE HANDLERS

Many air travelers have noticed that their luggage has been getting more of a bashing recently than it has in the past. This is no accident. Most airline luggage handlers must now go to school before an airline will allow them to touch a piece of baggage.

I was fortunate to visit the Dent Airline Luggage and Freight Handlers School in St. Louis last week. The Dent school trains most of the airline baggage handlers in the United States. Dent, the founder and president of the school, took me out on a large playing field the size of a football gridiron. Several classes were in session. The teachers all wore baseball caps and sweat shirts, and had whistles around their necks. The pupils were dressed in white coveralls. The first class we stopped to watch were throwing pieces of luggage to each other.

"All right, let's throw them a little harder," the coach yelled. "What are you guys, a bunch of cream puffs? You there, Pitowsky. You're not supposed to catch every bag. Drop a few."

Pitowsky dropped the next one, and it broke open, scattering clothes all over the field.

"Beautiful," the coach yelled. "Now you've got it."

"We use real luggage," Dent said proudly. "We simulate every possible situation a luggage handler will face."

"Ryan, you're catching the bags with two hands," the coach yelled. "You'll never break any that way. How many times have I told you to use only one hand when trying to catch a piece of luggage?"

We walked on down the field and came to a 16-foot tower. Several men were on the tower, dropping boxes marked FRAGILE to the ground.

"The object of this exercise," said Dent, "is for the men to get used to dropping fragile packages from great heights."

"But nobody's catching the packages," I said.

"Of course not." Dent chuckled. We went over to the coach who was inspecting each box after it dropped.

"Claremont," he yelled up to the tower, "these scientific instruments are still intact. What are you using for a throwing arm?"

"Threw them as hard as I could," Claremont yelled back.

"Well, put some spin on it the next time."

Claremont threw another box, and we heard the glass shattering. The coach nodded his head.

"Good boy."

The next group we came to was running an obstacle course. Pieces of luggage were strewn on the field, and the men had to jump from one piece of luggage to another without their heavy work boots hitting the ground. The hinges were broken on most of the bags and the locks were crushed.

"After running the hundred-yard course, stomping on the luggage," Dent said, "the men then have to throw a forty-pound bag fifteen yards, kick a cosmetic case twenty-five yards, and thrust a sharp object through a canvas suitcase, blindfolded."

"You're doing wonderful work here," I told Dent.

"When a man finishes our school," Dent said, as he picked up a broken camera that had fallen out of a bag, "he is certified to work as a baggage handler for any airline in the world."

SAINT RALPH'S IN THE SQUARE

It has been reported that the president of the Toyota Motor Company has had a half-million-dollar shrine constructed in Japan for the repose of the souls of people killed in Toyota cars.

The question that immediately comes to mind is: "Will the American automobile companies follow suit?" A gesture such as this, while not contributing significantly to auto safety, would certainly show the American public that the auto companies care.

The American automobile companies have two choices: One is to build an individual shrine for each make of car —"Our Lady of the Corvair," "The Latter-Day Mustang Tabernacle," "Temple Oldsmobile in the Vale," "The Little Chrysler Around the Corner" and "The Valiant Sisters of Mercy"—or one large shrine which would take in all the automobiles manufactured in the United States.

I would opt for one shrine with as many chapels as there are makes of cars produced in this country. It would probably have to take up hundreds of acres of land, but, built in a convenient location, the shrine would eventually pay for itself in parking fees alone.

So that one company wouldn't benefit more than another, the shrine would be named Saint Ralph's in the Square after Ralph Nader, the patron of safety in the United States.

A large statue of Nader being followed by a detective from General Motors would be erected in front of the shrine. The best American artists would be commissioned to paint frescoes on the ceiling, showing great moments in car crashes, and the aisles of the shrine would be paved in asphalt.

On each altar, in gold, would be the latest model of a car or bus produced by the manufacturer, and seats with safety belts would be provided for those who wish to meditate on the future of the automobile.

There would be services held twice a day for people

who died from pollution and others who expired while waiting for their warranties to be honored.

Music would be provided by the tire companies, and candles could be purchased with gasoline trading stamps.

Saint Ralph's in the Square would hold high holy services on the day the new car models came out, where anyone contemplating buying one would receive a special blessing.

A special chapel would be set aside for those people who wanted to pray that their automobile insurance would not be canceled, and a traffic commissioner would be on duty at all times to give absolution to those who had sinned on the highway.

Since it will be difficult for everyone in the United States to visit the shrine, it will be suggested that those people caught in traffic jams take a rug out of their car each morning and each evening and bow in the direction of Saint Ralph's in the Square.

HOW TO RUN A RAILROAD

It's hard for the ordinary citizen to understand why a $7-billion corporation such as the Penn Central railroad could declare bankruptcy.

But this isn't the first time it's happened. The Larchmont, Saginaw, and Tallahassee Railroad had a similar experience, and perhaps people will be able to understand the Penn Central situation if I explain what happened to the LS&T.

As everyone knows, the Larchmont, Saginaw, and Tallahassee Railroad was one of the most profitable in the country. It specialized in bringing coals to New Castle, Pennsylvania.

In exchange for this monopoly, the LS&T had agreed to haul commuters from the suburbs into the cities of Larchmont, Saginaw and Tallahassee. While this was not a lucrative business, it was the price LS&T had to pay for using government rights of way.

Some time back, an executive of LS&T suggested that

the railroad get into another business, just in case the day might come when nobody wanted coals in New Castle.

"What business?" the chairman of the board asked.

"Why don't we buy a chocolate cake mix company? It certainly complements the railroad business."

So LS&T took the profits from their railroad and, instead of investing in new equipment, bought a chocolate cake mix factory.

This was followed by the purchase of a latex bra company, which was followed by the takeover of a malpractice insurance company.

Every dollar the LS&T made from its railroading was poured into a new business venture. Before long, LS&T was making greeting cards, building skyscrapers, drilling for oil, and making a bid to buy the Panama Canal.

Meanwhile, the LS&T's railroad was starting to suffer. Freight trains kept colliding with each other (the computers that used to keep them apart had been taken over by LS&T's book and magazine division), and cutbacks were made in passenger service.

When pressed by the passengers for better service, LS&T responded by raising commuter rates and locking all the washrooms on their passenger trains.

A citizen's committee called on the LS&T's offices, which were now located in their 5,000-acre development known as Sky City.

The vice-president of LS&T's Commuter Complaint Department (he was really working in the company's Training Department as an intern) said, "We are sympathetic with your problems and would be happy to improve the service and install new equipment, but we need the money for a sulphur mining project we've just taken a lease on in Canada."

"You owe it to the commuters," someone protested.

"We owe more to our stockholders. But I'll tell you what I'll do. I'll recommend we put lights back on the passenger trains during rush hour. It will be an expense, but it will show we have the public in mind."

Unfortunately, the vice-president was overruled by the finance committee, and the passenger trains remained

81

dark. Meanwhile, the major cash flow from bringing coals to New Castle started to dry up because so many customers were unhappy with LS&T's service. Without cash LS&T was in serious trouble.

So they hired President Nixon's old law firm to get them a subsidy from the Defense Department. When the story broke, the Defense Department had to turn them down, and LS&T had no choice but to file for bankruptcy.

The LS&T Railroad is now in the hands of the receivers, but thanks to wise investments in other fields, the LS&T Holding Company (which had spun off the railroad when it realized it couldn't be drained anymore) is now worth $25 billion.

WHO NEEDS THEM?

The American railroads may be behind the times when it comes to serving passengers, but as far as their public relations are concerned, they are literally in the Space Age.

Some months ago, the American railroads hired Wally Schirra, the astronaut, to do their radio and television commercials for them. Schirra, in his sincere voice, tells us what a great job the American railroads are doing for each and every one of us and always ends his commercials with the same statement: "The American railroads—who needs them? You do."

I'm quite sure Schirra wouldn't make a commercial unless he believed in the product, so the only thing we can assume is that he hasn't taken a ride recently on a passenger train.

I would like to imagine what would happen if one of our astronauts took a ride from Stamford to New York during the morning rush hours.

"This is Penn Central Control. We are eighty-seven minutes late into takeoff and holding. How do you feel, Wally?"

"I'm freezing my tail off. Where's the train?"

82

"It's in New Haven and holding, Wally. Suggest you guys go into the waiting room."

Twenty minutes later: "Hello, Penn Central. I am now in the cabin of the train and holding."

"Wally, our engineers advise us that the lack of heat will not hurt the train, so we're proceeding with all systems go. 10-9-8-7-6-5-4-3-2-1 *blastoff!*"

Static, noise, explosions, static.

"Wally, where are you? Give your exact position."

"I'm still in the Stamford station. The coupling broke on the engine."

Twenty minutes later, Penn Central Control: "Wally, we're going to try it again. Here we go, 4-3-2-1 BLAST-OFF!"

"Hello, Penn Central Control. We're moving, we're moving! It's beautiful."

"What do you see, Wally?"

"Nothing, the windows are all fogged. But what a feeling. It's the most wonderful feeling in the world to be on a train and actually moving."

"Hello, Wally. We're going to go through Larchmont in the next hour or so. We want you to drink some water."

"Penn Central, there is no water on the train."

"Wally, the doctors advise us if you stay on schedule, you may not need any water. But don't use up much energy. Can you see Larchmont yet?"

"I think so. There seem to be frozen carcasses of passengers piled all over the station."

"That's Larchmont. Get some photographs so our people can study them."

For the next forty minutes Penn Central Control lost contact with the train and, when they raised it again, asked, "Wally, where are you now?"

"Somewhere in Harlem on a siding. Can you give me an estimated touchdown time at Grand Central?"

"Our computers indicate you should be in the terminal no later than twelve fifteen P.M. Do you know what you're going to say when you put your foot down on the platform at Grand Central?"

"I'm going to say, 'The American railroads—who needs them? You do.'"

"Good show, Wally, and we're all praying here for you to have a safe journey home."

THE WIVES OF COMMUTERS

Recently I wrote about an astronaut trying to get from Stamford to New York on a railroad commuter train. After the article, I received a letter from a lady on Long Island who said, "Why do you always write about the men who take the trains? Why don't you write about the wives who sit and wait for them to come home?"

So here goes.

"This is Walter Cronkite in New York giving you live coverage of the 5:06 from Penn Station to Garden City, Long Island. While three courageous men wing their way toward home, we will now switch to Mike Wallace at the home of Mrs. John Boyle."

"Thank you, Walter. This is Mike Wallace, and I'm standing in front of the small modest home of Mrs. John Boyle, wife of one of the three men who are risking their lives in man's never-ending search for new horizons.

"Inside the house with her are the wives of the other two men who have also taken the 5:06 from Penn Station, Mrs. Bill Lewis and Mrs. Terry Clyne. We hope to have them out here any second. As you can see, the neighbors have been keeping a vigil outside the house since the train left New York.

"Here they come. The neighbors are applauding. Over here, Mrs. Boyle, thank you . . . Mrs. Lewis, Mrs. Clyne . . . give them a little room, please.

"Mrs. Boyle, how do you feel, knowing your husband is on the 5:06 from Penn Station?"

"I'm very proud of him. This is what he has always wanted to do, and I have no doubts he'll make it home."

"But aren't you the slightest bit apprehensive?"

"No, I have complete faith in John. He's dreamed of being a commuter since he was a little boy, and I've always encouraged him because I knew he wouldn't want it any other way."

"What have you been doing while you're waiting?"

"Watching television, cooking, trying not to think about it too much."

"Thank you, Mrs. Boyle. Now I'd like to speak to Mrs. Lewis. Mrs. Lewis, you have three lovely children with you. Do they know their father is a commuter?"

"Yes, we have no secrets in our family. Even Tommy, who is six years old, is aware that his father is somewhere out there on a trip."

"At a time like this, how do you keep your spirits up?"

"Through prayer. The minister of our church is with us, and he has been a great inspiration to everyone. Also, we've been grateful for the letters and post cards people have sent us wishing us well. Everyone has been so kind."

"Mrs. Clyne, did you want to say something?"

"Yes, I'd just like to add that while John and Bill and Terry are getting all the glory, they couldn't make this trip without the thousands of dedicated Long Island railroad employees, as well as the wonderful management team, from Governor Nelson Rockefeller on down. If it weren't for them, there would never have been a 5:06."

"One last question and then I'll let you go back inside, ladies. I understand that President Richard Nixon called you at six thirty tonight. Could you tell us what he said, Mrs. Boyle?"

"He wanted us to know how proud he was of our husbands, and he said that if they made it home, he would like us all to come to the White House for a state dinner."

TROUBLE IN PARADISE

At first glance Tahiti and the surrounding islands live up to their reputation as being an earthlike paradise. But after a week you notice many things wrong.

It's sad to report, but Tahiti lacks many of the refinements that Americans are used to.

For example, during the ten days we spent in Polynesia there was not one smog alert. I kept inquiring about smog, but only got blank stares from the natives. The simple souls didn't even know what smog was, which shows you how far behind the times the Polynesians still are.

Another thing that struck me was the fact that none of the dancers out here is topless. The Tahitian dancers prefer wearing bras to going bare, and an American tourist can make a fortune selling photos of Los Angeles go-go dancers to the natives, who are shocked that we allow our women to dance with nothing on.

It takes a few days for an American to get used to dancers wearing bras, but after a while you stop staring and it doesn't bother you at all.

One of the things that strikes you about Tahiti is the noise, which is deafening. The wind blowing through the palm trees, the surf crashing against the coral, and the constant flapping of the sails in the breeze is more than a person can stand. It's no wonder after a few days of this that a person longs for the quiet and solitude of New York City or Cleveland.

Another thing that hits you is the lack of formality in clothing. The women out here are not even conscious that the midi is now in fashion, and they are still wearing their sarongs above the knees. They also insist on wearing flowers in their hair.

One is amazed to see men without coats and ties in restaurants and bars. A tourist can't help wondering what on earth the missionaries have been doing all these years.

I am sorry to report that when you leave the main island of Papeete, there is no television. The only entertainment available on Bora-Bora and Moorea and Raiatea is provided by the natives, who sing and dance until early hours of the morning.

It's hard to believe that any civilization can survive without Johnny Carson or *Laugh-In,* but somehow the Tahitians manage to do it.

At the same time, you can see the effects the lack of television has had on the natives. They have no idea which detergent contains the most active ingredients; they don't know which shampoo will add luster to their hair. They have no clues as to what works faster than aspirin, and they don't even know what mouthwash to use when someone accuses them of bad breath.

The only thing the Tahitians have going for them, as far as we could tell, is that there is no generation gap.

A young man does not argue with his father when he's told he can't borrow the outrigger canoe. A young girl must be in her hut by ten o'clock at night.

How do Tahitian parents manage to wield this control over their children? They attribute it to a secret Tahitian phrase that has been passed down through the generations. When a child asks why he cannot do a certain thing, a Tahitian parent always replies, *"No te mea ua parau vau mi tera."* Translated into English, it means "Because I said so."

SAVING THE RAILROADS

The question of what to do about American passenger railroads is still very much on the administration's mind. There is no doubt that the railroads are losing money on passenger business. If they had their druthers, they would just stay with freight. At the same time, the public's need for passenger trains, particularly commuter trains, is great.

What is the solution? Professor Heinrich Applebaum, who holds the Casey Jones chair of railroad philosophy at Pullman University, has come up with a radical idea that could save both the railroads and the needed passenger service.

Professor Applebaum says the solution to the problem can be found in large aluminum containers which are now being used for freight.

These containers are placed on trains already packed, and unloaded the same way. This saves companies money in freight handling, loss due to pilferage and breakage, and also saves time.

Applebaum claims there is no reason you can't use the same containers for people.

This is how it would operate: Let us assume that 150 people are going to take the 7:30 A.M. from Greenwich, Connecticut. When they arrived at the platform, they would be horizontally placed in the containers. (This would give everyone an extra hour's sleep to New York.) The container would be insulated, as well as air-conditioned.

When everyone was squeezed in the container, it would be sealed. Then a freight train going through Greenwich would stop and the container would be hoisted on board a flatcar.

The same thing would happen all along the way. Commuters in containers at Portchester, Rye and Larchmont would all be waiting to be picked up by the freight train.

When the train arrived at Grand Central Station, the containers would be taken off by cranes and opened on the platform, and everyone could go to work.

The reverse would happen in the evening, Applebaum said, except in this case, to break the monotony, the commuters would be loaded in *vertically*.

The beauty of the plan, says Applebaum, is that by using containers, railroads could cut the cost of a ticket from Greenwich to New York by $3.50.

They could also profit by the fact that they would not have to build new passenger trains, and they could eliminate the bar cars.

Psychologically, they wouldn't have to worry about customer relations, as the commuter service would be run by the freight department.

The big advantage of this is that once the railroads were able to legitimately treat passengers as freight, they would improve their service rather than try to discourage people from using the railroads.

Applebaum says that, at the moment, the container idea would only be practical on short runs, but he felt that as time went on, a method could be developed for long runs to freeze people in refrigerator cars and then thaw them out when they reach their destinations.

The Department of Transportation, which is trying to find a solution to the passenger train problem, has expressed great interest in the Applebaum plan. A spokesman for the department said:

"If nothing else, it could save the Penn Central railroad."

EARTH DAY

In the beginning God created man, which, according to all the latest birth control statistics, was a big mistake.

And Man said, "Let there be light," and there was light, and Man called this light fire, and at first it was used to warm him and let him cook his food and protect him from the wild animals. But Man discovered fire could be used to burn down a forest or burn someone else's hut or tree house or a witch at the stake or soft coal or oil, which made the air turn dark gray and black. And this made Man start to cough and his eyes to run and his sinuses to hurt. And Man finally said, "God, what are You doing to me?"

And after God made the rivers and lakes and streams and oceans, Man dumped all the refuse from the earth into the waters, and it killed the fish and the plants and even the oxygen, and the waters turned muddy and brown and smelled, and no one could drink from them or bathe in them or even sail in them. And finally Man shook his fist at the heavens and said, "For God's sake, knock it off."

And Man created the wheel, and this was good because Man no longer had to walk through the forests or up and down the mountains or to school. And then Man created the engine which turned the wheels, and Man no longer had to depend on animals to pull him on the roads and paths. And Man called the new creature automobile, and it changed the face of the earth, for Man was forced to cut down the trees and flowers and pour concrete on the land to accommodate the automobile, and drill into the earth and the sea to fuel it, and sometimes the ocean turned black and the air turned brown, and as the automobile multiplied there was less space to park it, and it was unable to move any faster than a horse, and Man behind the wheel screamed, "Good God, am I ever going to get home?"

And Man created the plastic bag and the tin and aluminum can and the cellophane wrapper and the paper plate and the disposable bottle, and this was good because Man could then take his automobile and buy his food all in one place and he could save that which was good to eat in the refrigerator and throw away that which had no further use. And pretty soon the earth was covered with plastic bags and aluminum cans and paper plates and disposable bottles, and there was nowhere left to sit down or to walk. And Man shook his head and cried, "Look at all this God-awful litter."

And Man learned to split the atom, and then he took what he learned and he put it in a bomb to defend himself from other men, and he set off the bomb to see if it would work, and it did. And Man was very pleased with himself because he was safe from other men, and this was good. But other men learned to split the atom, too, and they put it in their bombs, and so Man had to make bigger bombs, and the other men had to make bigger bombs, and the explosions put radioactive material in the air which got into Man's food and water and made that which was nourishing inedible and that which would quench thirst undrinkable. And again Man became very frightened and said, "God help us all."

But by this time God had had it, and He sent down word to His loyal servant, Ralph Nader: "Now, Ralph, the first thing I want you to do is build an ark and then. . . ."

THE NEW BREED

There's a new breed of pilot now flying our commercial airways, and he's becoming a menace to the peace and tranquillity of the traveler. The taciturn James Stewart type of pilot is being replaced by the extroverted David Susskind type who not only never stops talking but tells you a lot more about flying than you want to know.

In the old days of air transportation you hardly heard from the captain up forward. He might have told you when you were taking off and when you could expect to land, but outside of that, he spent his time flying the plane, which is the most anyone expects of his pilot anyway.

But now, because he's either lonely or bored, or because the public relations departments of the airlines are in charge of the crews, the captain does a complete monologue from the time you get on the plane to the time you land. This is how it goes:

"Hi, folks, this is your captain. Well, we're going to have a great flight today to LA. Your hostesses are Kitty, Patti and Sally; your copilot is George and your engineer is Harry and I'm Jack. I'm married and have three fine children—Hildy, Freddy and Lisa, and we live in Roslyn, Long Island. We have a swell house and we belong to the First Congregational Church.

"There are some clouds over Kansas City, so we'll just avoid Kansas City today, which is not a great problem because we can get to LA anyway. It's lucky we're not going to Montreal because they're really socked in there, and there's a hurricane off Puerto Rico. But that shouldn't bother us today.

"We had some trouble with the turbofram which delayed us a few minutes, but it's been fixed now. We really don't need the turbofram, but government regulations require that it be in working order, just in case the gyrowhizzit goes out, which is hardly likely.

"Now, when we get in the air, you're going to hear a change in pitch in the motors, but don't let that bother you. If you *didn't* hear a change, then you should be bothered. Ha-ha-ha.

"I'll be putting up my wheels as soon as I take off, and you may hear a slight thump, but don't be disturbed by it. You have to get those wheels up fast when you're taking off—otherwise you don't get the lift, and a plane this size needs all the lift it can get, believe you me.

91

"I can't see if the wheels are up or not, but I do have a red light on my panel, and if that red light goes on, I would, of course, abort the flight.

"We're second in line to take off. There are planes landing and taking off every minute, and while the traffic may appear heavy to you, they seem to have it under control. Once we get away from the airport, we'll be out of danger.

"Well, here we go . . . there—we made it. No red light. I'm getting a slight reading on my oil pressure gauge, but it doesn't seem serious.

"As we fly across the United States I'll point out every town and city to you, and even if you can't see it because of the cloud cover, it's real beautiful country. You people on the right, if you look down now, you'll see Interstate 5344 over by the river. Sorry you people on the left can't see it. I hope to be driving on it soon. I'm taking the wife and children out to visit her mother on my vacation in a couple of weeks.

"We're going to turn the seat belt sign off, but I'd advise you not to unbuckle your seat belt and walk around. You can get a great deal of turbulence up here, and without warning the plane could hit an air pocket and take a dive, though of course it's unlikely.

"The temperature outside is now eighty degrees below zero, so I guess you're all glad to be inside. Ha-ha-ha. Say, I heard one I'll bet you folks haven't heard. There was this little kid and the teacher asked him. . . ."

JAPANESE SST

The Japanese have put in a bid for the SST now that it has been turned down by the U.S. Government. A delegation from Tokyo is in the United States at this moment negotiating for the plans and equipment, and I was fortunate to speak to one of the members. His name is Hakai Samauri, and he told me that he thought the Japanese would be able to build two prototypes of the SST by July.

"How much do you think the planes will cost you?" I asked him.

"We estimate that each plane will cost seventy-nine dollars and fifty cents, but this includes color television at each seat."

"That seems awful low," I said. "The Americans claimed they couldn't build an SST prototype for less than a billion dollars."

Mr. Samauri said, "That is because the Americans are so far behind in miniaturization. We feel we can get everything down to size, which will cut costs immeasurably."

"But how large will your SST be?"

"About the length of this conference table."

"You're going to build a supersonic transport airplane the size of this conference table?"

"Well, it will be streamlined. We won't have corners on it like this table."

"But how many people will an SST of this size hold?"

"I can't give you a figure now, but we intend to miniaturize the passengers. If we can get them down to size, we could get between two hundred and two hundred and fifty people on board."

"That's amazing," I said. "Why didn't the Americans think of that?"

"Americans have always been taught to think big. We Japanese have always been taught to think small. If you will excuse my impertinence, I believe the American SST manufacturers did not proceed with their plans in a wise way."

"How do you mean?"

"They announced they were building a supersonic transport airplane at the very moment your country was more interested in mass ground transportation. Had Boeing said they were going to build a supersonic train, no one would have questioned it. After they built the fuselage, they could then have announced that their tests showed it wouldn't work as a train, but in order to save all the taxpayers' money invested, they would add wings and see if it would fly."

"It probably would have worked," I said. "Tell me, Mr. Samauri, will your SST cause ecological problems?"

"We have made studies and we can say that if you had five hundred Japanese SST's flying at one time, they would give off as much pollution as twelve pigeons at the Washington Monument."

"I must say," I said, "you people really have this all worked out. How many do you plan to make?"

"Probably only a million in the first year. We don't want to flood the market."

"Wait a minute," I said. "What about the dangers of a sonic boom?"

Mr. Samauri took a brown paper bag out of his pocket, blew it up and then, as I watched in amazement, smashed it with his fist. It went "pop."

He bowed and said, "You have just heard a Japanese sonic boom."

SOUTH PACIFIC

If I had my life to live all over again, I'd live it as the CIA man stationed in Tahiti. You get up in the morning and see if there are any ships in the lagoon. If there are, you write down their names on a piece of paper in code, stick it in an envelope addressed to an old lady in Salt Lake City (who forwards it to Washington), and you have the rest of the day to snorkel, spear fish, water-ski, sail, and drink sloe-rum punches with lovely school-teachers, airline stewardesses and the daughters of French planters who were born during World War II.

I met one of these chaps at the bar in the Hotel Tahara, which is set in a mountain overlooking the lagoon of Papeete. I immediately knew he was a CIA man because at exactly nine o'clock he faced the sea and started striking his Zippo lighter on and off, despite the fact he had no cigarette in his mouth.

When the bartender confirmed he did this every night, I decided the man either was a CIA agent or had just given up smoking.

He was surprised I had seen through his cover so easily. "Most people think I work for the *Encyclopaedia Britannica*," he said.

"Whom are you trying to signal?" I asked him.

"Our man over there on the island of Moorea. We haven't heard from him in over a year. I'm beginning to suspect foul play."

"How could that be?" I asked him.

"Émile Debecque, that's his name, was a French planter who knew Moorea like a book. We needed a coast watcher who would station himself there and report to us on any Japanese ships trying to sneak into the lagoon."

"But why?" I said. "The war with Japan has been over for twenty-five years."

"Every Japanese ship going east that pulls into Papeete is carrying television sets, portable radios, cameras and automobiles. We can tell by the tonnage of the ships just how hard hit the American economy will be. We have to know before the ships reach Hawaii and San Francisco, so we can adjust our domestic production schedules. It is more important to know where the Japanese ships are now than it was during World War Two.

"So we sent Debecque into the hills to watch for us. But we haven't heard from him, and I'm starting to think the worst. Every night I come up here and signal him, hoping he will signal back."

As we were talking, a girl came in the bar with shampoo in her hair singing, "I'm gonna wash that man right out of my hair." Two little native children followed her singing *"Dites-moi, pourquoi."*

"What's going on?" I asked Jack.

"That's Nelly Forebush. She was a Pan American stewardess who met Debecque one enchanted evening at the Bali Hai Hotel and fell in love. Nelly was from Little Rock, Arkansas. After she fell in love with Émile, she discovered he had two native children by a Tahitian wife. Nelly at first was horrified, as it was against everything she stood for. But finally she became so enraptured with the children that she quit her job with Pan American and

95

promised Émile she would look after them until he came back."

"What an idea for a musical," I said. "But why the shampoo?"

"That's the sad part of the story. Nelly didn't know Émile would be gone this long, and she went bonkers three months ago when the two kids drove her up the wall."

We'll take on any coffee in the house.

Compare the taste of Freeze-Dried Sanka® Brand Decaffeinated Coffee to any coffee you have in the house with or without caffein.

How can we make this challenge?

Because when we take out the caffein we also take out a lot of the bitterness. We leave you with a good, smooth-tasting cup of coffee.

Come on. Put up your coffee.

GENERAL FOODS

PUT ON A LITTLE MUSIC AND LET IT PLAY

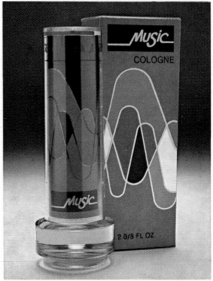

MUSIC—the lively new fragrance from Fabergé.
It's a song. It's a scent. It's a twist of lemon, flowered with wild geranium,
spiced with a whisper of Indian sandalwood and patchouli.
Put on a little MUSIC and let it play.
Cologne, Dusting Powder and Gift Sets—only 2.00 to 5.00.

5

THE GREAT AMERICAN RAT RACE

TOUGH CHRISTMAS HOLIDAYS

Christmas is getting to be tougher and tougher on parents of college-age offspring. Many students resent having to give up their holidays and spend them at home, and the holiday season, which was once an occasion for peace, joy and goodwill, usually turns into the battle of the generation gap, with the parents playing the role of General and Mrs. Custer.

My friend Random has a daughter named Kathy who interrupted her studies at Sarah Lawrence "to spend ten miserable days in Bethesda." (Her quotes, not mine.)

"It's hardly worth sending them the fare to come home," Random said as he sipped a beer. "Christmas seems to get them angrier than any other time of the year."

"How do you explain it?"

"Maybe it's the presents, or the fact that we're glad to see them. It really beats me."

"Lots of tension?" I said.

"We got along fine at the airport. There wasn't even a cross word while we were waiting for her luggage.

"It was when we got into the car and started driving home that things started to blow. Alice happened to mention that she had baked a lemon chiffon pie, which was Kathy's favorite when she was a child."

"Kathy got angry at that?" I said.

"Yes. She said, 'Oh, it's going to be one of *those* kinds of Christmases, huh?' "

Random sipped his beer again. "When we got home, we had signs up, WELCOME HOME KATHY. You wouldn't think something like that would upset a girl, would you?"

"I shouldn't think so," I said.

"She blew her top and said, 'Does everyone in the neighborhood have to know I've come home for Christmas?'

"Then we went in for supper, and the first thing Kathy wanted to know was what we were doing about Biafra. I admitted we weren't doing much about it, and she said

98

she suspected as much. She added it was typical of someone living in the suburbs not to think about Biafra. I promised her I'd get on Biafra the first thing in the morning."

"That satisfy her?" I asked.

"Not for long. Alice had fixed up the room just the way it was before Kathy left for school."

"Kathy should have been pleased," I said.

"Furious," Random said. "She said how could we expect her to live like this when the per capita income of people in West Virginia was three thousand dollars a year."

"The days and evenings must be very long," I said to Random.

"We've sort of worked out a schedule. Kathy sleeps until noon, then she has breakfast, then she gets on the phone. Then she waits for me to come home at six so she can have the car. One night I asked her if she wouldn't have dinner with us, and she replied, 'Do I have to spend *every* waking moment with my parents?' "

I bought Random another beer.

"Tonight I believe we're having a showdown," Random said.

"How's that?"

"We've given Kathy a new car for Christmas."

I said, "That wasn't a smart idea."

"We probably made a mistake, but we ordered the car before Kathy came home. How could we have guessed that a gesture of this kind would alienate us from her forever?"

DINNER FOR ONE

You don't see as many fathers and sons dining out as you used to. The problem seems to be that not many restaurants are set to handle some of the clothes their clients' sons are wearing.

The other night my friend McGrory suggested to his

son, Marshall, that they go to a first-class restaurant to celebrate his graduation from high school.

"Great," said Marshall, "let's go."

"I think you'd better put on a shirt," McGrory suggested.

"I have a sweat shirt on. What's wrong with it?"

"I thought you might put on a shirt and a tie," McGrory said.

"What are we going to, a wedding?" Marshall demanded.

"Most good restaurants prefer you to wear a tie," McGrory said.

"What for?" Marshall demanded.

"So you can get soup on it!" McGrory shouted. "Now put on a shirt and tie and don't give me any lip."

McGrory's wife came rushing in. "What's all the shouting about?"

McGrory said, "I'm taking him to Paul Young's restaurant for graduation, and he won't even put on a tie!"

"I don't want to go if I have to wear a tie!" Marshall yelled.

"Put on a tie," Mrs. McGrory said. "And a coat, too. Your father wants to be proud of you."

"What does putting on a shirt and tie have to do with him being proud of me?"

McGrory shouted, "It isn't that I want to be proud of you. It's just that I don't want to be ashamed of you!"

Marshall came down in a few minutes with a wrinkled shirt and a torn tie on. His face was red.

McGrory was just about to leave the house when he looked down.

"You have no shoes on," McGrory said.

"You didn't say anything about shoes," Marshall said. "Why do I have to put on shoes?"

"It's a health regulation!" McGrory screamed.

"Nobody's going to see my feet," Marshall protested. "They'll be under the table."

"Someone will see your feet as you're escorted to the table. People get very upset when they see a customer without shoes walking in a good restaurant."

100

"But it's summer. *No one* wears shoes in the summer."

Mrs. McGrory said, "Marshall, go upstairs and put on some sneakers. Your father asks so little of you."

Marshall stomped upstairs. "I didn't want to go to a restaurant in the first place."

He came down a few minutes later and got into the car and didn't say anything.

"Marshall," McGrory said, "would you take the red band off your head before we go into the restaurant?"

"What kind of place are we going to where they won't let a guy wear a band on his head?"

"It's a very good place, Marshall. They have fine food. You're growing up now, and you should be interested in other things besides milk shakes and french fries."

"You mean they don't have milk shakes and french fries at this place? I thought you said it was a good restaurant."

"Marshall," McGrory said quietly, "you see that McDonald's hamburger stand? Well, here's two bucks. You go over there and have anything you want for your graduation."

"You coming?" Marshall said.

McGrory shook his head sadly. "No, you'd only be ashamed of me."

A DIVORCE INSURANCE PLAN

The British are considering a plan to provide women with divorce insurance. The idea is that since marriage is getting more hazardous all the time, women should be protected in case their husbands can't support them and the children after the marriage is dissolved.

If the plan is adopted and is successful, there is no reason why divorce insurance in the United States would not become a big thing.

This is how it might work:

An insurance agent for the Niagara Falls Marriage Casualty and Life Insurance Company would scan the engagement notices of his local newspaper. Then he

101

would select a likely prospect, perhaps Miss Mary Philpott of Roxbury, Connecticut, who has just announced her engagement to Mr. Seymour Rocks of Philadelphia.

The agent would call on Miss Philpott with a bouquet of red roses.

"Miss Philpott, I read in the newspaper this morning that you are going to marry Mr. Seymour Rocks, and I wish to offer my heartiest congratulations."

"Oh, thank you. I'm so happy, I'm flying. Who did you say you were?"

"Nate Bienstock of the Niagara Falls Marriage Casualty and Life Insurance Company," he says, handing her his card.

Miss Philpott says, "Thank you very much, but I don't need any life insurance."

"I'm not selling life insurance, Miss Philpott. I'm selling divorce insurance."

"You've come to the wrong person." Miss Philpott giggles. "Seymour and I will be married forever."

"Forever? Are you so certain?"

"Of course I'm certain. We're madly in love, hopelessly, endurably, unforgettably."

"Miss Philpott, for your sake I truly and sincerely hope that everything you say is true. But our statistics, kept up to date by our own computers, show that your marriage has one chance in three of being dissolved in the next seven years."

"Not my marriage, Mr. Bienstock. Not with a wonderful man like Seymour."

"But you're only seeing the good side of Seymour now. Wait until you're married. Miss Philpott, in every Seymour Rocks, there's a Joe Namath screaming to get out: a Seymour who will spend his evenings with the boys, a Seymour who will sit every weekend watching football on television, a Seymour longing and yearning for his carefree bachelor days. This divorce insurance policy was written for that Seymour, not the one who put a diamond ring on your finger."

Miss Philpott is almost in tears.

"Seymour is forever," she cries.

"That's what Liz Taylor said about Eddie Fisher, Miss Philpott, that's what Zsa Zsa Gabor said about Conrad Hilton, and that's what Jean Peters said about Howard Hughes."

"But how can I buy divorce insurance before I'm even married?" Miss Philpott asks.

"That is what your Niagara Falls Casualty agent is here for. To help you plan ahead. Now, we have some very good all-inclusive policies, including one in case you break up in a foreign country."

"How much divorce insurance should I get?" Miss Philpott asks, sobbing.

"Well, from what you've told me about Seymour being such a swinger and scoundrel, I'd advise you to take the maximum."

THE HENPECKED FATHER

The days when a husband came home to a henpecking wife are a thing of the past. In these perilous times, it isn't a man's wife who gives him hell, but his children.

I didn't realize how common it was until I ran into my friend Nolan in a bar around six o'clock in the evening. Nolan was belting them down pretty fast and I said to him: "Don't you think it's about time you went home?"

"What for?" Nolan said. "I'll just catch it from the kids."

"Have they been hard on you lately?" I asked.

"They're impossible. The minute I walk in the door they start in on me. Why do they have to wait for dinner while I watch the news? How come I can drink a martini and they can't smoke pot? Why can't they each have a telephone in their own room? I tell you, they're driving me crazy."

"Why don't you tell them to shut up?"

"I do, but it doesn't do any good. They're so deaf from listening to their records that they can't hear anything I say. If they've had a fight with their mother and I stick

103

up for her, they all accuse me of taking her side. I can't seem to do anything right.

"I have a seventeen-year-old son, and he's the bomb thrower in the family. He says everything in the system stinks. He's ashamed of the bourgeois life we lead and the bourgeois friends we have and the bourgeois job I have. But he's not above borrowing my bourgeois car to drive his girlfriend to a student meeting to overthrow the bourgeois establishment."

"It must be tough," I said to Nolan, buying him a drink.

"When my sixteen-year-old daughter goes out on a date and I say she has to be in at a certain hour, she says I'm destroying her social life, and it will serve me right when she winds up on a psychiatrist's couch."

"They really put you through the wringer, don't they?" I said.

Nolan was practically in tears. "You don't know what it's like. The other night my thirteen-year-old said that Paul McCartney of the Beatles was dead. I said he wasn't dead—that it was all a put-on, and that he was alive and well in London. She said I didn't know what I was talking about, because all the kids knew he was dead. I showed her a picture in the newspaper of McCartney, proving he wasn't dead, and she said the grown-ups were just hiding the facts from the kids, because we wanted them to think he was alive. She said if I lied to her about McCartney, I probably lied to her about everything."

"What's the answer, Nolan?" I asked as I bought him another drink.

"If it wasn't for my wife, I'd probably call the whole thing off. I love my wife, and I wouldn't do anything to hurt her."

"Then you're keeping the marriage going because of your wife?"

"That's all that's left of the home. I'm putting up a front with the kids, just so I can be near my wife. But it isn't easy. It's so hard for a wife to live in a house where there is bickering going on all the time, and I think she senses that the only reason I come home at night is because of her."

"But, Nolan, you can't stay married just because you love your wife," I said.

"It's tough," he said. "But I can't make her suffer just because I have three kids that drive me up the wall."

THE GREAT AMERICAN RAT RACE

One of the complaints the kids voice today is that parents put too much pressure on them. I accidentally listened to such a discussion the other evening at Goldfarb's house.

Young Goldfarb, aged sixteen, told his father he saw no reason to study such irrelevant subjects as math, language, science, history and English.

"Who needs it?" young Goldfarb said.

"You need it," his father shouted.

"Why?" young Goldfarb demanded.

"Because of Springfield. If I don't push you, Springfield's kid is going to get ahead of you in school. How would you like that?"

"Who cares if Springfield's son gets ahead of me?" young Goldfarb said.

"Springfield does, that's who," the older Goldfarb replied. "Oh, wouldn't he love it if he could say his kid was doing better than Goldfarb's."

"You mean to say you've been leaning on me all this time because you're in a contest with Springfield?" young Goldfarb said.

"I didn't start it," the older Goldfarb said. "It was Springfield who began pushing his kid first. Years ago, I heard Springfield tell his kid, 'Never take second best. Go for all the marbles. Get out in front and show them what you can do.'

"When I heard this, I had no choice but to make you work your tail off. If you're mad at anyone, you should be mad at Springfield."

"But Springfield's kid doesn't want to compete with me any more than I want to compete with him. Why don't

I call him up and tell him if he knocks off beating his brains out, I'll knock off beating my brains out?"

"That would be just fine," old Goldfarb said. "But what about Ascarelli's kid?"

"What's Ascarelli's kid got to do with it?"

"You think Ascarelli is going to stop pushing his kid just because you two let up? And how about Bernheim's son? Bernheim has already announced his kid is going to Yale. You want Bernheim's kid to go to Yale and you wind up at some community college in Florida?"

"But don't you understand, Pop?" young Goldfarb said. "Ascarelli's son couldn't care less if he got ahead of us, and Bernheim's son doesn't give a damn whether he gets in Yale."

Old man Goldfarb got up and took his son over to the window and pointed out to the flickering apartment lights across the Potomac.

"If it was just *one* Springfield or *one* Ascarelli or *one* Bernheim, I would say, 'Enjoy yourself; don't break your back.' But out there, where you see those lights, are thousands and thousands of Springfields and Ascarellis and Bernheims, and do you know what they're saying to their kids tonight? They're saying, 'The only thing I want you to do is to *beat Goldfarb!*'

"All over America, the Springfields, Ascarellis and Bernheims are vowing to beat you out of a job, a sale, a taxi, a contract, a home, a wife. And do you know why they're doing it?"

"No," said young Goldfarb. "I don't know why."

"Because at this very moment they know I'm telling you to get them before they get you."

"But if you stop, maybe they will," young Goldfarb said.

"It's too late," the older Goldfarb said. "Springfield, Ascarelli and Bernheim are too ambitious for their sons to quit now. So be a nice boy and go do your homework."

6

THE ENEMY COW

THE BIG POKER GAME

The bullet-scarred Indochina Bar and Grill was jammed when the dusty stranger walked up and ordered a straight whiskey.

"You doing a big business," the stranger said.

"Yup," the bartender replied. "We've been expanding at a furious rate."

"What's the crowd doing over there?"

"They're playing poker. The game's been going on for eight years now, without a stop. It started as a little domino game, but pretty soon it escalated into poker."

The stranger wandered over to the table. There were six men sitting around the table—Black Jack Hanoy, Tiger Cy Gone, Charlie Cong, Big Sam, Little Louse, and Kid Kamboadia.

"Who's winning?" the stranger asked a man named Frenchie.

"Beats me," he said. "I quit playing with these guys sixteen years ago."

Big Sam had a giant stack of chips in front of him, and he kept giving chips to Tiger Cy Gone after each hand.

Frenchie whispered, "Big Sam says he wants out of the game, but he won't quit until Black Jack Hanoy admits defeat. Black Jack just sits there with a poker face, and every time his stack gets low the Chinese guy and the fat guy they call the Bear give him more chips to play with."

"What are the guns doing on the table?" the stranger asked.

"Each player says the other guy is cheating. We've had some big shoot-'em-ups around here. I've seen some mean poker games, but this beats all."

"How did it all start?" the stranger asked.

"Wal, way back before anyone can remember, Charlie Cong and Tiger Cy Gone started a penny ante poker game among themselves. Pretty soon Tiger Cy Gone, who was one of the worst poker players around, began losing, and so Big Sam, who was considered one of the great card-players of all time, started to give the Tiger advice. Big Sam also staked Cy Gone to a small stack of chips, which the Tiger lost immediately. So Big Sam gave him a larger stack, and Tiger Cy Gone, who couldn't get the hang of the game, lost that stack.

"Finally, Big Sam got so exasperated that he decided to get into the game himself. He put a large stack of chips in front of him hoping to scare Charlie Cong out.

"But instead, Charlie called on his friend Black Jack Hanoy, who was anxious to get in the game because he had a grudge against Tiger.

"Before anyone knew it, the game escalated from penny ante poker to table stakes with one winner. Big Sam figured that with all his chips he could bluff and Black Jack Hanoy would have to fold.

"But Black Jack Hanoy was being backed by the Chinese guy and the Bear because they had a grudge against Big Sam.

"So now the stakes are really high, and nobody is going to admit he lost."

"What are Little Louse and Kid Kamboadia doing in the game?" the stranger asked.

"They were just two spectators watching, but Black Jack Hanoy and Big Sam made them sit in. Little and the Kid don't even know how to play poker, and they're both broke; but Big Sam says the more players there are in the game, the more chance Tiger Cy Gone will have of winning, and the sooner Big Sam will be able to go home."

As they were talking, Big Sam dealt the cards. "Okay," he said, "this is the big hand. If we win this one, we'll win all the marbles."

Frenchie whispered to the stranger, "He keeps saying that every time he gets the deal."

BULL

There is no problem at the Pentagon in organizing bombing and strafing raids in Indochina. The real difficulty is what to call them.

A special section of the Defense Department has been set up to supply the Secretary of Defense and his spokesmen with various alternatives to describe the air war in Indochina.

Every morning, promptly at eight o'clock, the committee which is called BULL (Bureau for Lethal Logic) meets to discuss what the day's raids will be called.

A typical meeting goes something like this:

"We've got twenty B-52's bombing Cambodia today. What do we say we're doing?"

"We're interdicting enemy supply routes from the North?"

"We said that yesterday. Why don't we say the strike is a defensive measure to speed up the Vietnamization program?"

"We used that phrase three days ago to explain why our helicopters were supporting Cambodian troops."

"Why don't we say we're bombing North Vietnam to enhance the Nixon policy of speeding up the withdrawal of American boys from Vietnam?"

"That's not bad. But it would be stronger if we announced the raid was made to wipe out Communist sanctuaries that were being used to build up an offensive which is expected to be launched after the rainy season."

"How would we say it?"

"We could say that our air operation in Cambodia was being conducted to limit the enemy potential before they can bring it to bear effectively against friendly forces in the area."

"That's beautiful, General. No one's ever put it that way before."

"This may sound as if it's coming from left field, gentlemen, but I thought we might blame Congress for the raid. The Secretary could announce that all he was doing was following the letter of the law which was passed by Congress to support any action by the President that would bring our American boys back home."

"It's worth running up the flagpole, Colonel."

"One of the people in my office had a unique suggestion. He thought we might announce that the B-52's were not bombing in Cambodia but were just making a defensive ordnance drop on fixed enemy positions."

"I like the sound of that. Let's write it down before we forget it."

"Has anyone thought about saying that we were neutralizing a free-fire area?"

" 'Neutralizing' is a good word. It has an innocent ring to it."

"I don't want to top you, but what if we said we were neutralizing Cambodia to protect its neutrality?"

"Wow. That's got everything in it."

"I know you guys think I'm a hard-liner, but I think we should stop beating around the bush and announce we're bombing the hell out of Cambodia to kill as many dinks as we can, so the dirty Red s.o.b.'s will become true believers."

"You want the Secretary of Defense to say that?"

"Why not? That's what we're doing, aren't we?"

"General, wash out your mouth with soap and water."

RICE—THE ULTIMATE WEAPON

Left-wingers and limousine liberals have been quibbling about the success of our incursion into Cambodia. While there has been some question as to how many weapons we captured and how many sanctuaries we wiped out, there is absolutely no question that we captured the largest rice supply dump in Southeast Asia.

Pictures of this rice have been shown on television and distributed to the press. According to intelligence reports, the invasion of Cambodia was worth it for the rice alone.

The administration has claimed to have seized 51,000,-000 pounds of rice, which is the equivalent of 102,000,000 cups of rice, which breaks down to 1,632,000,000 billion tablespoonfuls, which was enough to make rice pudding for every man, woman and child in the Vietcong.

The problem, after we captured the rice, was what to

111

do with it. We couldn't leave it in Cambodia because we had to pull out on June 30, and the rice might have wound up on the black market. Trucking it back to Vietnam was suggested, but that could get the Mekong Delta Rice Growers Association up in arms, particularly since Cambodia grows a better grade of rice than Vietnam.

American GI's hate rice, so there is no sense trying to make it part of their diet. And if we give the rice to the Lon Nol government, it may be embarrassing because rumor has it he sold the Vietcong the rice in the first place.

Showing pictures of captured rice on American television does have some propaganda value, but if you show too many sacks of it, people will start wondering if that's all we got out of our assault on Cambodia.

A solution to the problem has been suggested by a Los Angeles lawyer named Arthur L. Martin, who studied the subject at Rice University in Houston, Texas.

Martin discovered that rice expands four times its size when it is cooked. He believes that the rice we captured in Cambodia should be dropped into Haiphong harbor, where it would swell in the warm waters and block the harbor.

Bombing Haiphong harbor with rice would not be considered an act of war because the U.S. Air Force could claim it had dropped the rice on a mercy mission to Laos and had missed its target.

No ships could get in and out of the harbor once it was clogged with Cambodian rice. Hanoi would scream and shout in Paris, but international law would be on our side. We could prove that every grain of rice we dropped in the harbor came from a Cambodian Communist sanctuary.

Martin estimates it would take thirteen months to dredge the Haiphong harbor of rice, and by that time, if the Cooper-Church Amendment isn't passed, we could go back into Cambodia and find more rice to drop in the harbor.

While the Pentagon refused to comment officially on the Martin Haiphong Saturated Rice Bombing Plan, one general, with the Joint Chiefs of Staff told me, "We're always ready to try anything."

SCHWARTZKOPF'S WAR

The year 1997 will go into history as the year the Vietnam conflict became known as Schwartzkopf's war. President Nathaniel Schwartzkopf certainly didn't start the Vietnamese war. He inherited it from President Zimmerman when it was called Zimmerman's war. President Zimmerman inherited the war from President Luther Bainbridge, who was defeated for a second term when his opponents tagged Vietnam "Bainbridge's war."

This was unfair because President Bainbridge had gotten stuck with the war when President Samuel Goodbody announced he would not run for a second term if people didn't stop calling it Goodbody's war.

President Goodbody had history on his side because when he took office, it was known as Plotnick's war, after President Ezra Plotnick. President Plotnick, if you recall, had promised if elected he would go to Saigon. It was this trip that caused the press to name the war after him.

Before President Plotnick, the Vietnam hostilities were known as Fowler's war in honor of President Whitney Fowler, who promised to have the American boys out of Vietnam by Shirley Temple's birthday.

He obviously failed to meet the timetable; but observers at that time admitted that President Fowler was not at fault. He had taken on the task of finding a solution at the time it was known as Agnew's war. President Agnew took over the war when President Nixon decided not to run in 1972, because everyone called it Nixon's war. He said they should have known it was "Johnson's war."

President Johnson, in one of his rare interviews at the LBJ ranch, muttered it should have been called Kennedy's and Eisenhower's war.

In any case President Nathaniel Schwartzkopf, who won a close election in 1996 by promising the electorate that he had a solution to the Vietnamese war, ran into

113

the same difficulty that other Presidents had. Hanoi was being adamant in Paris, and, according to President Schwartzkopf, the United States had gone as far as it could in finding a just and fair settlement.

For example, President Agnew had offered the North Vietnamese Saigon and Hue. President Fowler had said if Hanoi was willing to talk peace, they could have Thailand and Cambodia. President Plotnick stood by President Fowler's offer and threw in Indonesia, the Philippines and Japan.

But Hanoi's negotiators in Paris said it was just a trick to make them settle.

To show his good faith, President Goodbody, when he took over, said that he would let the Vietnamese have Australia as well. This might have broken the ice in Paris, except that Australia got wind of it and leaked the story to the press. Once it was in the newspapers, Hanoi said it had been hoodwinked by Goodbody and called off negotiations for six months.

Then, through neutral diplomatic channels, President Bainbridge, who knew his political career was at stake, sent word that if the North Vietnamese would accept even a cease-fire, they could have Switzerland.

Hanoi was tempted to accept this proposal, except that President Nu Twang of South Vietnam held a press conference and said that he would never agree to Switzerland becoming part of North Vietnam.

In order to placate President Nu Twang, Bainbridge said that if South Vietnam permitted Hanoi to have Switzerland, the United States would give the Saigon government Sweden.

Before President Nu Twang could give his reply, Hanoi rejected the U.S. offer in hopes they could get a better deal by waiting for President Zimmerman to be elected.

But President Zimmerman failed miserably, and it is now President Schwartzkopf's turn. He got off to a good start by promising Hanoi, if they agreed to a settlement, they could have all the land in the United States west of the Mississippi.

But a bulletin just in from Paris says that Hanoi has turned the proposal down.

THE SCIENCE OF BODY COUNTS

One of the things that constantly impresses people in Washington is the accuracy of the body counts in Indochina. No part of the war has been handled with as much scientific accuracy as enemy-body counting, and we know to the last Commie aggressor how many Vietcong have been killed each day.

The Office of Enemy Body Counts is located in the Pentagon and has a staff of 23,678 people. The director of OEBC is a civilian named Hammersmith Moody, who could safely be called the father of enemy-body counting.

"When the war was first started," Moody said, "body counting was a hit-or-miss proposition. Our boys would go into an area, shoot up the place, burn down the village, and then phone in a figure of enemy killed to Saigon. This figure was arrived at by questioning each GI who was in on the operation and asking him, 'How many gooks did you get?'

"Now, almost every outfit in Vietnam had soldiers from Texas in it, and no matter what the other GIs said, the Texans would insist they got more. So everyone kept escalating the figures, and pretty soon there was some question as to how accurate the count was. To further complicate matters, the South Vietnamese troops found out the easiest way to please the American high command in Saigon was to hand in high enemy-body counts.

"The more enemy the ARVN commander could report dead, the more equipment, medals and promotions he could get for himself and his outfit, and pretty soon South Vietnamese officers were flooding Saigon with exaggerated body-count statistics."

"There doesn't seem anything wrong with that," I said. "After all, no one got hurt."

"True," Moody said. "The complication arose, though, when these figures were reported to the Pentagon and

115

released to the public. At the rate we were reporting enemy deaths, we would have run out of anyone to kill in the first sixteen months of the war. How could we justify our staying in Vietnam after we had reported that everyone in North Vietnam was already dead?"

"It isn't easy," I admitted.

"So I was asked to develop a new body-count system which would make it possible to prove that we are beating the Communists, at the same time guaranteeing there were enough left to make us keep our commitment."

"How did you do it?"

"We took all the counts submitted by the various units and divided by six.

"But even this figure was too high to announce every day, so we set up what could be called an enemy-body-count bank. Now when things are going bad and the press and public are getting restless, we release figures from the bank which will prove how well we're doing in Vietnam."

"Are you doing the same thing in Cambodia?" I asked.

"The emphasis in Cambodia has been on supplies rather than bodies, but we're still getting very high reports from the field. If we can report ten enemy dead for every ton of rice seized, we'll be very satisfied."

"Don't you have a recognition problem in Cambodia? How do you know when you see a Cambodian or North Vietnamese body that it belonged to the enemy?"

Moody replied, "Through dental charts."

APPLEBAUM'S LATEST PLAN

Despite President Nixon's and Vice President Agnew's attempts "to bring us together," the country still seems to be divided on the Vietnam and Cambodia issues.

There is, among young people, a lack of confidence in President Nixon's methods of disengaging us from Southeast Asia. On the other hand, the majority of Americans still support the President's hard-line strategy, particularly since they don't have to go.

Professor Heinrich Applebaum, of the Institute of

Retribution and Conciliation, has formulated a plan that may satisfy both groups in this country.

The professor told me, "My studies show that there are far more people in this country who are for what Nixon is doing in Vietnam than are opposed."

"That's wonderful."

"The only trouble is that the people who are the President's strongest supporters are too old to be drafted into the Army."

"It figures," I said. "What is your plan?"

"My plan is very simple. We must make it possible for those who are for us being in Indochina to go there and fight, and those who are opposed to us being there to come home."

"You mean we should raise the age limit for men to be drafted into the service?"

"Not raise it. Abolish all age requirements so anyone who believes in the war can ship out immediately."

"What an ingenious plan!"

"My studies," the professor said, "have indicated that there are hundreds of thousands of people who have said to our young citizens, 'I only wish I were your age so I could fight.' The Applebaum plan makes it possible for these people to get their wish."

"But maybe they didn't mean it," I protested. "Maybe they just said it to make the kids feel better."

"Of course they meant it. Do you know of one person who wouldn't give up his soft job if he could slog through the rice paddies of the Mekong Delta?"

"It's hard to think of one," I admitted.

"The beauty of my plan is that you would have a tough determined type of soldier who would go right into the breach, without question."

"Just as in the Charge of the Light Brigade," I said excitedly.

"Eventually, the U.S. Army would only be composed of people who sincerely believed that what we were doing in Indochina was correct."

"You could call it the Love America or Leave It

117

Brigade," I said. "How do you plan to recruit these people once the age requirements are waived?"

"We'll ask for volunteers. If that doesn't work, we'll go through President Nixon's mail. Anyone who wrote supporting his policies would automatically be drafted."

"Professor Applebaum, you have come up with the most brilliant solution to an untenable situation. The way you describe it indicates that no one could object to your plan."

"It's foolproof, if I must say so myself," said Professor Applebaum. "With the men who support Nixon manning the front lines and the men who oppose him back here in the States, we could stay in Vietnam for twenty years, and no one would give a damn."

PLANE TALK

No one is quite certain if and when the United States will sell Israel the 125 fighter planes it's been asking for. The rumor in Washington is that the policy for the moment will be not to give Israel any new planes, but to replace those shot down by the enemy. If this is true, we can expect to see a decided change in the communiques emanating from Tel Aviv and Arab capitals.

They may go something like this:

TEL AVIV, July 10—Military spokesmen for the Israeli air force announced today that their planes were attacked along the Suez Canal. Twenty-seven Israeli planes were shot down, the spokesman said, and 30 more limped back to their bases. This was the largest loss of Israeli combat aircraft ever recorded.

CAIRO, July 11—Egyptian army officials angrily denied shooting down any Israeli planes in yesterday's battle over the Suez Canal. "Our pilots," said General Gamal Emer, "missed the Israeli planes by miles.

"We have aerial photos showing all Israeli planes returned safely without so much as a bullet hole in them."

General Emer said he was also very disappointed in the new Russian-type SAM missiles which failed to hit the Israeli attackers. "It's apparent there is no hope we will ever shoot down an Israeli plane."

HAIFA, Israel, July 15—A sneak attack along the Syrian border by Israeli fighters proved to be a catastrophe, Israeli sources said today. The high command revealed that Syrian planes had shot down 23 Israeli fighters, bringing Israeli losses for the week to 50 planes. General Mordacai Rashnik has been relieved of his command for allowing these defeats to take place.

DAMASCUS, July 16—Syrians demonstrated in the streets today against Israeli claims that Syrian fighter planes had shot down 23 Israeli planes in yesterday's dogfight over the Golan Heights.

At a giant rally in Damascus Square, Arab nationalist leaders introduced several Syrian pilots who claimed they had turned tail as soon as the Israeli planes approached.

"We did not engage them in battle," Lieutenant Abdullah Yafed told the screaming crowd. "The Zionist pigs did not lose any planes. They shot down five of ours."

The crowd cheered this news and then burned down the Jordanian Embassy.

TEL AVIV, July 25—Prime Minister Golda Meir went on Israeli television tonight to regretfully announce that 30 more Israeli planes had been shot down by French-built Mirages over Libya. This was the farthest penetration Israeli planes had made. When it was pointed out after the broadcast that France had not yet delivered the Mirages to Libya, Mrs. Meir said, "I made a mistake. Our planes ran out of gas."

AMMAN, Jordan, July 26—King Hussein demanded today that the United Nations take over the counting of Israeli planes lost in action. Charging Israel with duplicity, the king said, "We can never have peace in the Middle East as long as Israel keeps claiming plane losses it has never had."

CAIRO, Egypt, August 1—President Nasser and the Soviet military command announced jointly that all Arab planes had been grounded indefinitely and all antiaircraft guns had been silenced until further notice, to prevent the Israelis from announcing any more plane losses.

SOMEWHERE IN THE NEGEV, August 2—Foreign correspondents today were taken on a guided tour of this top-secret Israeli air base in the Negev. The base, which is the home of 45 fighters, was completely empty of aircraft.

A reporter asked where the planes were, and the colonel in charge of the tour said, "They were all lost this morning to small-arms fire over the Dead Sea."

When it was pointed out that Israel has claimed to have lost 125 planes in three weeks, the exact number it had requested from the United States in the first place, the colonel replied, "Oy—what a coincidence."

THE ENEMY COW

I have no intention of passing judgment on Lieutenant Calley. But when I read that one of his defense attorneys said that Calley had been ordered to kill *"everything"* in Mylai, including livestock and *"every living thing,"* I became intrigued. So I sought out a friend of mine at the Pentagon and said:

"Look, why would anyone be ordered to kill livestock?"

"Those were Vietcong cows," my friend said defensively. "We knew for a fact that the cows at Mylai had given milk to Vietcong soldiers. Those cows can't claim they didn't know what they were doing."

"But maybe they had no choice," I protested.

"Two weeks before we went into Mylai, we sent helicopters with loudspeakers over the area, warning everyone to get out. Those cows heard us, and they refused to leave. Therefore, we concluded that the cows were sympathetic to the Communist cause."

"What about the chickens and the pigs?"

"The same thing goes for them. Our intelligence revealed that the chickens had been laying eggs for the Vietcong for years. They were red hens."

"What about the pigs?"

"The pigs were worse than the chickens. When we went into the village, we found warm pork still cooking in the pots in some of the huts."

"The only way Charlie could have got that pork was from Mylai pigs. When our men realized where the pork was coming from, they went berserk and decided to shoot every pig in sight."

"But the ducks. Why were they ordered to kill the ducks? They weren't even from Mylai."

"In a war, innocent livestock have to be killed. You can't say to men going into battle, 'Kill the cows, kill the chickens, kill the pigs, but don't shoot at the ducks.'"

"It seems like such a waste of food."

"You people sitting back here in your comfortable offices in Washington can say you should kill this or you shouldn't kill that, but when you're out in the field, it's different. You don't have time to ask, 'Is this a good cow or a bad cow? Is this chicken a local chicken or was he brought down from the north to feed Charlie? And that innocent-looking pig walking across the road. What is he really thinking?'"

"Then what you're saying is the only good cow is a dead cow?" I said.

"You could sum it up that way. When we go into a village, we assume everything on legs is working for Hanoi. Sure you make mistakes. But it's still better to err than to let a chicken get away and come back to haunt you on another day."

"I imagine you can't spare dogs either," I said.

"When we say every living thing, we mean every living thing. If you make exceptions, the example will be lost on the Vietcong. The one lesson we've learned from Nam is to let every living thing know that if it helps the enemy, someone is going to pay for it. I'm sure after Mylai that the cows in other villages are going to think twice before they give milk to Charlie."

THE LOVED ONES

THE JOBLESS PATRIOT

There has been a great deal of discussion by the government concerning unemployment. No one likes to be without a job, but it seems to me that if you explain it to someone in terms that he can understand, the unemployed person will be willing to go along with it.

"I beg your pardon. Is that a pink slip in your hand?"

"Yeah."

"Well, congratulations. You can consider yourself a front-line soldier in the President's fight against inflation."

"I can?"

"Yes, sir. And under government regulations you are entitled to a complete explanation as to why you find yourself in what we refer to as the 'unemployment-rate zone.' Incidentally, you will be happy to know that your being laid off came as no surprise to us."

"It didn't?"

"No, sir. Your government predicted that, given high interest rates and a tight money situation, you would be out of work by February. Here it is, right on the graph."

"I'll be darned. You guys really know your stuff. But what do I tell my family?"

"You can tell them that although they will have to put up with a certain amount of inconvenience, the upward spiral in unemployment—to which I might say you've made such a valuable contribution—will have a very definite effect on the stabilization of prices."

"They'll be happy to hear that."

"If it weren't for people like you, I'm afraid the economy would have kept overheating and your dollars would have lost their purchasing power. But if we can raise the unemployment level to a reasonable figure, say four and a half percent, without putting the country into a recession, we can bring prices down by 1975."

"It makes sense to me, but I would like to ask you a question. Am I better off reversing inflation by being unemployed, or am I better off working and earning dollars that have less value?"

"That's the kind of question that we in the government resent. I would say in the short run you might be better off earning inflationary dollars. But if you're truly concerned about the economy of the country, then you should be willing to be part of the four and a half percent of the population that we need on our unemployment rolls."

"But why me?"

"Everyone says, 'Why me?' It has to be *somebody*. If we are to take strong anti-inflation measures, we have to have a citizenry ready to make financial sacrifices. All we're asking of you is to stay unemployed until the economy cools off."

"How long will that be?"

"We're projecting eighteen months, but I'd count on two years to be on the safe side."

"What am I supposed to do in the meantime?"

"This is a Certificate of Unemployment, which you can hang on the wall. It attests to the fact that your government appreciates all you are doing to keep the economy from spiraling sky-high."

"Gosh, it's beautiful."

"I might mention that only the elite of the labor force in this country is entitled to this certificate. You can be very proud that you are among the chosen few."

"Wait until my family sees it. Is there anything else I can do to help fight inflation?"

"Just stay off the streets. And don't call us. We'll call you."

WHY SUCCESS SPOILS
GOVERNMENT GRANTS

Despite everything you hear about the government, there still is plenty of money around for projects. The only trouble is, you can't get the money if you have a plan that works. You must have one that no one is quite sure about.

A vice-president of a university system in the Northeast told me about this the other day when he applied for money for a program to run summer schools for students who needed extra help to get into college. He told me the meeting went something like this:

"Now, Mr. Haas, from our records it appears that you're applying for a grant of five hundred thousand dollars to run a summer school project for students hoping to keep up in college this fall."

"That's correct. We did it last year, and it was tremendously successful. We only had a dropout rate of six percent."

"Oh, dear me. Then this is not a pilot project."

"No, it's not. We know it works."

"What a shame."

"What do you mean what a shame?"

"Well, if this were a pilot project, the government would be happy to finance it. We'd be very interested in knowing what could come of it. But we can't very well give money to something that's been proven, can we?"

"Why the hell not?"

"Mr. Haas, we're very willing to fund any educational program, providing it's iffy. But we can't throw money away on things that work. Congress would have a fit."

"I still don't understand why."

"I'm trying to explain it to you. The government has no trouble getting money from Congress for study programs. It doesn't matter how much it costs to study a program; we can get the funds. But once we ask for money for a program that has been proven successful, Congress will be committed to it, and nobody wants that, do they?"

"Suppose that I request the money for a study project. Could I get it then?"

"But you already told me that it had worked last summer. There's no sense having a study of it if it works."

"I'm not trying to be difficult, but this is a very important project. We are taking in people this year who are going to find it tough sledding to keep up in the fall unless they have some remedial work."

"It's not our fault that your program worked last summer, Mr. Haas. Had it failed, we would have given you a blank check to try it a different way. But we're not here to dole out taxpayers' money for programs that have succeeded.

"Just the other day a superintendent of a public school system in the Midwest tried a visual-reading program for his state which turned into a disaster. The machines didn't work, the teachers couldn't handle them, and the students lost interest after the first five minutes.

"Did we cut him off? We did not. We gave him another ten million dollars to find out why he failed. And we're ready to pour in another ten million dollars if he doesn't come up with answers. The whole department is excited by the failure."

"Is there any possible way of getting the five hundred thousand dollars, knowing what you know about my program?"

"I hardly think so, Mr. Haas. You've made a mess of things as it is. Our motto in the government is: Nothing fails like success."

THE CASE AGAINST EDELWEISS

The dismissal of Rory Edelweiss from the Internal Revenue Service has been upheld by Bureau 1040, as well as 1040A of the IRS, and has been confirmed by Clark Mollenhoff, the White House assistant in charge of income tax returns.

Edelweiss has become a *cause célèbre* in taxpayer circles because he tried to simplify the federal tax form, much to the horror of everyone in the Department of the Treasury.

His supervisor, Glenndenning Hindsight, said that the IRS was perfectly right to fire Edelweiss.

"He was a troublemaker," Hindsight said, "and could have destroyed the entire tax-collection system in this country."

"What did Edelweiss try to do?"

"He tried to write a tax form that the average taxpayer could understand."

"What on earth for?" I asked.

"Who knows what goes on in a mind like that? Some think he was working under too much pressure. Others say if he had been given a test when he was six years old, we would never have hired him.

"In any case, Edelweiss came to us eight months ago with a simple tax form which anyone could have filled out. He had eliminated references to forms 2440, 3903, 2106 and 2950SE, and such phrases as 'see tax rate schedule three on T-1 and tax table B on T-2.' "

"What did you do?"

"We thought he was joking at first. But Edelweiss said he was dead-serious. He had worked on the return for over a year and felt that the implementation of it could cut down the taxpayer's work to three hours."

"I hope you told Edelweiss where to get off," I said.

"As his immediate superior, I tried to talk sense into him. I told him that if we simplified the present federal tax form so people could understand it, they might decide not to pay their taxes. The real purpose of a complicated tax return form was to wear the taxpayer down, so by the time he finished making out the return, he was so exhausted he would be willing to pay whatever he had to, just to get the return out of his house."

"He must have seen the logic in that," I said.

"Edelweiss was adamant. He said under his system the tax forms were so simple that he could save the country the 1,700,210,000 man-hours of work which are now devoted to filling out the 1040 return.

"But I told Edelweiss that if God wanted the American people to have a simple tax return, He would have created one for them. He wouldn't budge, so I had no choice but to turn him in to the authorities."

"They must have been upset when they heard Edelweiss was trying to make a tax return that anyone could understand."

"Absolutely furious. The IRS has a staff of fourteen hundred people who do nothing but complicate the income tax forms. Whenever they discover that an item is comprehensible, they immediately take it out and replace it with something so vague and confusing that no one will get it. When they heard one of their own people was trying to simplify the life of the taxpayer, they considered it treachery of the first order."

"So he was fired?"

"We made an example of him. After what we did to Edelweiss, it's going to be a long time before anybody comes up with any bright ideas on how to save the taxpayer his sanity and time."

PUBLIC LIBRARY ENEMY NO. 1

The most important thing to remember this year is not to look back: because Big Brother is catching up to you.

The latest Orwellian news to hit the American public is that Treasury Department agents representing the IRS are visiting public libraries to check on what books readers are taking out.

The investigators are interested in anyone who has borrowed books on explosives, but their interest also includes anyone who might be checking out "militant and subversive" publications as well.

The checks have been confirmed by the IRS, and a spokesman, when asked about it, said, "As far as I know, it's just routine. The only thing special is some librarian complained about it."

It's good to know the IRS is concerned with the rights of its citizens. But at the same time it's going to make those of us who use the public libraries think twice before we take out a book.

I can imagine a scene at the Maplewood County Public Library.

"Miss Philpott, my name is Spangle and I'm a Treasury agent with the Internal Revenue Service. Have you noticed anything suspicious around here lately?"

"Suspicious?"

"Anyone taking out any funny books?"

"Let me see. Someone borrowed Robert Benchley's collection yesterday."

"I don't mean that kind of funny. I mean books about explosions, stuff like that."

"Come to think of it, Harold Flemingheimer took out *Chitty Chitty Bang Bang* and hasn't returned it yet."

"*Chitty Chitty Bang Bang,* huh? What does this Harold look like? Does he have long hair?"

"Oh, yes."

"Sloppy dresser?"

"I should say so. He comes in here without shoes on."

"You don't have a duplicate of his library card, do you, Miss Philpott?"

"Yes, I do. He lost his and we had to issue him a new one. We found the old one. Here it is."

"Hmmnn, very interesting. He took out *The Little Red Fire Engine* on May sixth, *Three Little Pigs* on May twentieth, and *Joan of Arc* on June twelfth. Has he ever talked politics with you?"

"Not really. He's only nine years old."

"Well, keep an eye on him. Do you mind if I go through your files? Who is this Philip Crestwood who took out *The Guns of Navarone* on April twelfth?"

"He goes to Columbia University."

"He does, does he? I notice on July first he took out *Gone with the Wind.*"

"Is there something wrong with *Gone with the Wind?*"

"Don't you recall the burning of Atlanta?"

"Of course. I never did like Philip Crestwood. He forgot to return *Thunder Out of China* last winter and he was fined fourteen cents."

"Well, Mr. Crestwood is going to go into our little computer. These people always make tiny mistakes that trip them up. Being a member of the public library might result in Mr. Crestwood's downfall."

"Are you going to go through all the cards?"

"If you don't mind, Miss Philpott. Unbelievable as it may sound to you, Trotsky learned everything he knew from the Odessa Public Library Branch No. Two."

LIVING ON THE PLANTATION

It's hard for people who do not live in Washington, D.C., to imagine what it is like to survive in a town where you are not permitted to govern yourself. Even the citizens of Saigon have more to say about their affairs than we do.

In order to understand what it's like, you have to imagine Washington as a huge plantation with 1,000,000 tenant farmers. Up on the hill are the plantation owners made up of Congressmen from Virginia, Kentucky and South Carolina.

When the farmers want something, a delegation of poor whites and blacks climb up the hill to the great marble house, with their hats in their hands, and a spokesman says, "Massuh, our people down there wants a subway. Can't get around anymore without a subway, boss. Any chance us getting a subway, please?"

The plantation owners are very paternalistic, and, in spite of their picture, none of them carries a whip. They laugh a lot.

"Now, what you all want a subway for? You been doing fine all these years without a subway."

"Yassuh, boss, but things getting rough down there. It's hard for people to get to work without a subway. Plantation is getting bigger all the time, boss. We sure could use a subway mighty bad."

"You folk down there are never satisfied, are you? We been good to you, haven't we, boy?"

"Yassuh, boss, you treat us jus' fine. We is about the happiest tenant farmers in this here country. But we sure need that subway, boss."

"Subways cost money, boy. Money doesn't grow on trees. If we build a subway, we're going to have to take profits from the plantation and tax you more for your land."

"That's true, boss. But since we been paying taxes anyway, we'd just as soon have a subway."

"Well, as you know, we plantation owners have the

131

best interests of our tenant farmers at heart. We really don't see why you people need something as worthless as a subway, but if that's what you want, we'll try to get you one."

"That's mighty gracious of you, boss, mighty gracious. I was telling people down there in the cotton land, all we got to do is ask the owners and they'll give us a subway."

"Of course, we'll want something in return. This is a big favor we're doing you."

"Don't have to tell us that, boss. What can we do for you?"

"We'll give you your subway, if you agree to us building a road to Maryland right through the northeast part of your land."

"But, boss, you build a road through there and you're going to tear down everybody's home. People won't have any place to live."

"That's not our problem, boy. We need that road so folks can get out to Maryland. That road's a lot more important to us than your people's subway."

"Not wishing to show any disrespect, boss, but we can't go back and tell our people they have to have their houses torn down so we can have a subway."

"That's too damn bad about you people, but we decide up here what you can have and what you can't have."

"We know that, and if it was up to us, boss, we'd let you have your road to Maryland. But those farmers down there are sick and tired of everyone pouring concrete on their homes."

"This is our plantation, and we'll do with it what we see fit. You tell us once more you don't want a road to Maryland, and we'll cut you all off from the general store. Now don't come back with any more talk about a subway until you're willing to talk about a road."

"Thank you, boss. You've been most generous with your time. God bless yuh, suhs. God bless yuh."

HOW TO SPOT AN
UNDERCOVER AGENT

In the past we saw fifteen FBI agents drop out of the John Jay College of Criminal Justice in New York because a professor made critical remarks about J. Edgar Hoover, the FBI's stalwart leader.

Following this, eleven FBI employees were ordered to drop out of the course on "Violence in America" at American University because the professor there cast aspersions on Mr. Hoover's leadership.

There will probably be more of this as time goes on, and it is conceivable that every university in the country could soon be on J. Edgar Hoover's blacklist.

What isn't generally known is that there is a conspiracy among university professors to criticize J. Edgar Hoover publicly.

This is why they're doing it:

It is assumed that the FBI has planted undercover agents in all the major universities in the country. These undercover agents look exactly like radical students. They have long hair, wear beards, go shoeless, and use all the obscene words. In the past they have been impossible to spot on campus.

But not long ago a professor at a Midwestern college made some derogatory remarks about J. Edgar Hoover. Three of the radical students immediately walked out of the class in a huff. Everyone was very surprised when they announced they were leaving the school.

It turned out they were FBI undercover agents, whose job it had been to infiltrate the radical movement.

They had been ordered to put up with any indignity to win the confidence of the radicals, *except* to sit there and take criticism of Mr. Hoover.

A few weeks later in California, a professor in government statistics made the point that the higher the crime rate rose in the United States, the more kudos J. Edgar Hoover received from Congress and the administration.

The professor was trying to show that bad news does not necessarily bring criticism from government. He said that as far as his statistics showed, there hasn't been a year when the FBI did not report a rise in crime in the United States, and each time it did, Mr. Hoover received congratulations from the President.

Two radical students in his class broke into tears and announced they could no longer stay in school. It was a blow to everyone because one of the undercover agents had just been elected president of the SDS and had been in charge of an anti-war demonstration in Governor Reagan's office.

Well, these two incidents suddenly made professors all over the country realize that the easiest way to spot an FBI undercover agent was to criticize J. Edgar Hoover.

And so professors are now waging a campaign to make remarks about the head of the FBI.

The FBI knows, of course, what is happening, but they're caught in a bind. If they keep their agents on campus to catch the people responsible for student violence, they will be exposing FBI employees to defamatory remarks about Mr. Hoover.

So far, the FBI has left it up to the individual agents to decide whether to stay or leave. But they're proud that in every case so far when someone has sullied J. Edgar Hoover's name, the FBI undercover agent has indignantly dropped out of school.

EASY RIDER

There has been a lot of criticism of Congress for not doing enough work this year. I believe that if any criticism should be levied at Congress, it's that it has done too much work. There isn't a bill proposed these days that doesn't have seven riders attached to it which have nothing to do with the legislation that is being proposed.

This can be illustrated in the case of Jan Klopinski, a refugee from Poland who was trying to get American citizenship. Because of red tape, Jan could not get his

American citizenship through normal channels, and so he got his Senator to propose a private bill to make him a citizen.

It is done all the time and usually goes through without any difficulty. But this year, any bill in Congress is subject to amending, and as soon as the Jan Klopinski bill for American citizenship was proposed on the floor, a dove Senator got up and added a rider calling for the repeal of the Gulf of Tonkin Resolution.

This angered several hawks in the Senate, and they added a rider of their own which would give Chiang Kai-shek four squadrons of B-52 bombers.

A Senator from Louisiana then proposed that a rider be attached to the Klopinski citizenship bill raising the oil depletion allowance to 35 percent. He immediately was followed on the floor by a Senator from North Carolina who wanted the bill amended to take all health warnings off cigarette packages.

The rumor started spreading that the Jan Klopinski citizenship bill was in trouble.

No one knew how much trouble until a liberal Senator added a rider raising Social Security payments by 50 percent. This was followed by another rider from a Midwest Senator raising salaries of postal workers by $100 a week.

The White House, which hadn't been paying much attention to the Klopinski bill, suddenly got to work and called Minority Leader Hugh Scott over for breakfast. Senator Scott was told the President was very displeased with the Jan Klopinski citizenship bill in its present form.

When Senator Scott reported this back to the Hill, everyone decided to get into the act.

A Senator from South Carolina added a rider forbidding federal judges from ruling in desegregation cases. A Senator from Arizona added a resolution recommending the President resume bombing of North Vietnam. A Senator from California proposed a rider making it a felony to boycott grapes.

Meanwhile, Jan Klopinski had gone out and bought a new black suit for the swearing-in ceremonies. Because of his limited English, he had no idea that his bill was in so much difficulty until President Nixon decided to go on television and appeal directly to the American people.

The President said, "I want to make it perfectly clear that I am for the Jan Klopinski bill for American citizenship, but only if it does not cause inflation, or a sellout in Southeast Asia. I appeal to every American who is part of the great silent majority to write to his Senator today and tell him you support my position on Klopinski."

Vice President Agnew went on television two nights later and attacked the three networks for discussing the Klopinski bill before Americans had a chance to digest the President's message.

In the meantime, two more riders had been tacked onto the bill, one authorizing the building of ten nuclear aircraft carriers and the other making marijuana legal.

The bill was finally passed with all the riders intact. Unfortunately, President Nixon decided to veto it and Jan Klopinski, through no fault of his own, lost his opportunity to become a citizen of the United States of America. He sold his black suit and took the next boat to Australia.

FITZGERALD'S BLUNDER

A. Ernest Fitzgerald, who blew the whistle on the overruns for the Air Force's C-5A airplane, was fired from his $28,900-a-year job. The Pentagon said it was eliminating the cost-analysis position as an economy measure and not in retaliation because Fitzgerald told Congress the plane would cost $2 billion more than the Lockheed Aircraft Corporation had estimated.

I was inclined to be sympathetic with Fitzgerald's position until I heard the Air Force's side of the story.

I have a friend at the Pentagon who said everyone missed the point.

"We didn't eliminate Fitzgerald's job to save $28,900," he said. "We eliminated the job because Fitzgerald was costing us millions."

"How's that?"

"Well, his job was to reduce costs and achieve economy in Pentagon purchasing. He was supposed to study contracts, watch budgets, and see that the military was not overcharged. As long as he did this without coming up with any irregularities, we could live with him. But the minute he thought he discovered waste and inefficiency and Congress found out about it, he cost us a packet."

"I don't understand."

"Well, take the C-5A as an example. Once Fitzgerald revealed that the bill on the plane would be two billion dollars more than originally anticipated, the Air Force had to go into high gear to defend its procurement methods.

"We had to take five generals, as well as hundreds of civilians, off other projects to develop testimony justifying the two-billion-dollar overrun. We had to fly up Lockheed executives from Marietta, Georgia, for conferences on the best way of explaining the added costs.

"We had to go to great expense having charts made, position papers printed, and press releases mimeographed. We were forced to hire public relations experts to keep the name of the Air Force from being sullied by ax-wielding Senators.

"The entire defense budget was in jeopardy, and we had to spend thousands of dollars lobbying on the Hill. It was a frightening experience for everyone."

"And Fitzgerald was responsible for all of it?"

"Certainly he was. Had he not come up with the disclosures, the Secretary of Defense and the deputy secretary wouldn't have had to have a big advertising campaign proving the value of the C-5A. All in all, we estimate that, with the man-hours and other costs, Fitzgerald cost us over a million dollars to defend the plane. So when the smart-aleck press says we're trying to save $28,900, they don't know what the hell they're talking about. Getting rid of Fitzgerald's job saved the American taxpayer a million dollars."

"I don't think we should sniff at that," I said.

"Fitzgerald meant well, but he just didn't understand how costly his revelations would be. He didn't see the big

137

picture. He didn't understand that with the Air Force, as with all the military services, it's much more expensive to defend a mistake you made than to let the mistake go by unnoticed."

"It's obvious from what you've told me," I said, "that he didn't have the taxpayer's interests at heart."

"We hope, if nothing else, that this will be a lesson to our other cost-management people."

AN ARMY THAT LISTENS

The Army has been accused of investigating and keeping files on civilians, including Senators, Congressmen and leading citizens. I couldn't believe this was true until I happened to be passing through a basic training camp the other day and I saw a crusty drill sergeant holding up a tape recorder. He was talking to a platoon of recruits.

He barked, "Now this is your M-134 Field Issue Tape Recorder. You will carry this tape recorder at all times. This tape recorder is issued with three F-107-X cassettes, which you will carry on your belt ready for instant loading when you are in a combat situation. Any questions so far?"

"What constitutes a combat situation, Sarge?"

"A combat situation during which you would use your M-134 Field Issue Tape Recorder could occur at a political convention, a peace rally, a university lecture, or if you were sent on patrol through the halls of Congress.

"Now, your M-134 Field Issue Tape Recorder can pick up sound at two hundred yards, providing you use this B-62 directional microphone. You must assume that anyone you have been ordered to follow is the enemy, so you will record first and ask questions later. Your M-134 Field Issue Tape Recorder has been designed so you can tape at night as well as you can in the daytime. It must be cleaned after each bugging and recharged for use the next day. Any questions?"

"Sarge, suppose we're out trailing a Senator and we

run out of tape. Do we return to base or do we continue following him?"

"You will be working in pairs. One man will be sent back for more tape, while the other will continue pursuing his quarry. But I want to warn you to use your tape *only* when you have the enemy within earshot. Don't fire until you see the whites of their earlobes.

"Now, you will wear your M-134 Field Issue Tape Recorder under your jacket in this holster, like so. This will leave your hands free to take photographs of the enemy with this P-140 Cigarette Lighter Automatic thirty-five mm Camera. This P-140 CLA thirty-five mm Camera may save your life. While recording your enemy, you will shoot him or her automatically. It has proved its value in hand-to-hand surveillance at the Republican and Democratic conventions.

"You will each be issued twenty rounds of Tri-X film to go with your camera. This will enable you to wipe out a rock festival, an anti-Vietnam demonstration or the governor of a state. Any questions?"

"Suppose we're trying to get near a governor and he's too far away?"

"You must ask for air support. The Air Force will take photos of the situation, and they will also try to pick up any conversations that you missed. Any questions?"

"Suppose we're out in the bushes of a Cabinet officer's home tapping his telephone and we're discovered. What do we do then?"

"You will give nothing but your name, rank and serial number. The Geneva Convention protects you if you are captured while tapping any U.S. government official's telephone.

"Now we're going out to the obstacle course on Capitol Hill. Half of you will pretend to be Congressmen, and the other half will track them down with your tape recorders. I want this platoon to realize the stakes are high, and while this may seem like just an exercise, what you hear and see today may win the war against civilians. I don't want anyone coming back from patrol and saying he has nothing to feed into the Army's computers."

THE LOVED ONES

This is a government of reports and studies. No matter what happens in this nation, the first solution is to appoint a commission to study it. The commissions take one year, two years, some even longer, and then they make their report to the President. If the President agrees with the report, it's released to the nation. If he or his staff disagrees with it, it's buried. But where?

Just by chance I discovered the secret burial grounds of reports and studies made by Presidential commissions. The cemetery is located on a hill overlooking the upper Potomac. It is quiet and deserted, and only the chirping of birds or the call of a hoot owl can be heard.

Mr. Gottfried Snellenbach has been caretaker of the burial area for government reports since the Harding administration, and after I assured him I would not dig up any of the graves, he let me enter the large well-kept grounds.

"We've got some of the great reports of all times buried here," Mr. Snellenbach said. "We've got reports that cost twenty million dollars, and we've got reports that cost two thousand dollars, but in the end they all wind up here, buried six feet under."

"Sir, what kind of reports are resting here?"

"It might be better to ask what kind of reports aren't buried here. We have reports on violence, studies on blacks, students, unemployment, the economy, the Communist threat, housing, health care, law and order. You name it, and we've buried it."

"How does a report find its final resting spot in this setting?"

"Well, as you know, the President is always appointing a commission to study something or other, and after the study they're supposed to hand in a report. Now, lots of times the President has no intention of paying any attention to the report, and it's dead before it's even written. Other times someone on the President's staff reads a re-

140

port handed in by a commission and says, 'This stuff is dynamite. We have to kill it.'

"In some cases the President says, 'Let's release this report to the press and then bury it.' Occasionally a report will just die of heartbreak because nobody pays any attention to it.

"In any case, after the report is dead, it has to be buried, because if you're President, you don't want someone finding it at a later date and using it against you.

"So every week each report that has died is placed in a pine box and loaded on a government hearse and brought up here, where we have a simple ceremony before lowering it into the ground.

"If it's a blue-ribbon panel report that's been killed in action, we give it a twenty-one-gun salute. Otherwise, we lay it to rest with as little fuss as possible."

"This cemetery goes for miles and miles," I said.

"No one knows how many reports have been buried here by the different Presidents."

"Mr. Snellenbach, this is a beautiful cemetery and very impressive. But why does the government go to so much trouble and expense to keep it up for nothing more than paper reports?"

"You must understand that most of the men asked to serve on Presidential commissions are very important citizens. They spend months and years working on these reports, and they feel very close to them. When their reports are killed or buried, these men feel a personal loss. Many days you will see them sitting here next to the tombstones of their studies, tears rolling down their cheeks. No matter how long you work here, it still gets to you."

8

MIDI ÜBER ALLES

MIDI ÜBER ALLES

It was the end of the 1970 fall fashion season, and the news on all fronts was bad. The Führer, deep down in his bunker underneath the Seventh Avenue subway, was reading reports from all parts of the country in rage and frustration.

"Mein Führer," one of his aides told him, "Seventh Avenue is in ruins. The midi-length skirt has bombed. All is lost. We must surrender."

"Don't tell me we have lost the war," the Führer screamed. "We will counterattack. We will punish all those who refuse to wear the midi-skirt!"

Another aide came in. "Good news, *mein* Führer," he said. "Bonwit Teller reports it has just sold two midis today."

The Führer started to dance a jig. "You see, swine. It is selling! The midi is selling! Today, Bonwit Teller . . . tomorrow, the world."

The Führer went over to his map and stuck two pins in it. "That makes two hundred and thirty-four midi skirts sold this year. I told you the women would go for it."

Another aide came in with a telegram. *"Mein* Führer, Saks Fifth Avenue has surrendered to the mini forces. So has Macy's, Gimbels and Bloomingdale's. We cannot hold out much longer. Perhaps we should issue a communiqué saying that it makes no difference what length a woman's skirt is this year as long as she's happy."

"Never! Never!" screamed the Führer, kicking over chairs and tables. "I decreed that women would wear midis and they will wear midis, whether they like them or not."

The aides looked at each other in hopelessness. The Führer's mistress, who was playing solitaire, looked up from her game, "Perhaps it may be better, *Liebchen,* to give in."

The Führer looked at his mistress and screamed, "Yes, and if I surrender, I will be tried as a war criminal and they will hang me. They will say I brought ruin to all of them. The answer is no. My plan to bring order to the fashion world will triumph. If they do not listen to me, there will be anarchy in the land. What word from Sears, Roebuck?"

An aide came in with the new Sears, Roebuck catalog.

"They've replaced the midi with pants suits," the aide said.

"Traitors! They will pay for this," the Führer yelled as he started tearing the catalog to bits. "I made Sears, Roebuck, and I will destroy them."

The telephone rang and an aide grabbed it. "Yes, yes. Good, good." Then he turned to the Führer. "It's Orbach's. They have a customer in the store and she's looking at midis."

The Führer started to dance another jig. "The tide is turning," he cried.

"What's that?" the aide said. "Oh." He hung up the phone. "Her husband came in and dragged her out of the store."

The Führer's mistress began to cry. His Alsatian dog, sleeping in the corner, whined.

The teleprinter rang.

An aide went over to the machine. "I. Magnin's, Marshall Field, Lord & Taylor, and J. C. Penney have collapsed. They're all holding fire sales on the midi."

The Führer sank down in his chair. "That does it. No more Mr. Nice Guy."

The Führer's mistress took a bottle of cyanide capsules out of the drawer and placed one in each cupcake. Then she called over the dog and gave him a cupcake. He ate it eagerly and rolled over dead.

She poured out two cups of coffee. She handed the Führer a cupcake. He looked at her and said, *"Liebchen,* you believed in the midi, didn't you?"

The mistress took the other cupcake. "With my legs, what choice did I have?"

NO FUN AT THE FUR FARM

The maxi fur coat has put a terrible strain on all our furry animals. Everything from mink to raccoons is in tremendous demand, and it is impossible to fulfill all the orders. I didn't realize how serious it was until I visited a fur farm in Upstate New York. I talked to a male mink named Emba who seemed to be very tired.

"It's been agony," he said, wiping the perspiration away from his forehead. "The farm is on a full twenty-four-hour shift, but we still can't meet the demand. Stand in front of me so the farm owner doesn't see I'm resting."

Emba said, "It was bad enough when they introduced the maxi fur coat for women, but what really did it to us was when they started pushing maxi fur coats for men. There's just so much a mink can supply."

I believe I detected a teardrop in his eye.

"This used to be a wonderful farm," he said. "We worked hard in the summertime to supply the pelts for fall and winter, and then we could take it easy. You know, play and roll around and rub noses, the stuff minks like to do. But then the furriers went crazy. They got into a fur-price war. They started dyeing furs in crazy colors; they made fur pants, fur blouses, fur *après*-ski outfits; they put fur on fur. The fur farms were besieged with orders. We were told to produce minks or else.

"Every time the farmer sees me resting, he starts measuring my pelt with a tape measure. What choice do I have?"

"It must be hard on the female minks, too," I said.

"They hardly get to feed their offspring before they're expected to produce a new family. The farmer has installed loudspeakers which play music that is supposed to make our work easier, but in between the music he puts on commercials, such as 'An idle mink is a dead mink' and 'The mink paw you save may be your own.' "

146

"It must be difficult to give birth under those conditions," I said.

"The driving force behind every fur farm now is fear," Emba said.

"It isn't just us," he continued. "Look at those rabbits over there. Would you believe at one time those rabbits were happy at their work?"

"They seem so listless and haggard," I said.

"When a rabbit doesn't want to be a rabbit, then you know the fur craze has gotten out of hand," Emba said.

"Are those beavers over there?"

"They used to be eager beavers, but even beavers have a breaking point. They're so tired reproducing other beavers they don't bother to build dams anymore. You see that male beaver walking on all fours? Would you believe he's only one year old?"

"This place certainly is depressing," I said.

"I don't know how much longer I'm going to last," Emba said. "I've fathered one hundred and thirty-four mink babies, but it's getting to me.

"My back isn't what it used to be, and I have pains in my shoulders and I don't sleep well anymore.

"If you would just send out the word that even minks have their limits, you would be doing everyone here a favor. It may be too late for me, but perhaps my sons and their sons would be spared what I've had to go through since the maxi fur coat became the fashion of the year."

GUNG HO

It could be the war or all the talk about revolution, but the latest fashion craze in the country is a cartridge belt for women.

I discovered this the other day when I went into a store to buy a present for my wife.

The salesgirl took me over to a rack where there were belts of bullets in all sizes.

"This is the latest thing in accessories," the girl said. "Your wife would love one."

"I was hoping for something more in a hand grenade," I said.

"Believe me," she said. "Women are just crazy about these bullets. They can wear them around their chests or around their hips or let them hang loose like this."

"You don't have anything in tear gas, do you?" I asked her.

"Now, you're not being serious," she said.

"I don't know how to tell you this," I said, "but my wife is a dove."

"All the more reason for buying her a bullet belt," she replied. "It's better to *wear* bullets than to shoot them."

"But I was in the service, and I don't know anyone who wore a belt of cartridges who didn't eventually want to shoot them."

"These are dummy bullets," she said, "and all the powder's been taken out of the casings."

"But what's to prevent another store from selling powder to go with the belts?"

"Nothing," she said, rather irritated. "But even if a store sold powder for the bullets, you would still need a machine gun to fire them."

"What would prevent a handbag manufacturer from making a bag that could turn into a machine gun?"

"It's ridiculous," she replied. "If a handbag turned into a machine gun, all the contents in the bag would fall out."

"I never thought of that. What are you featuring in flame-throwers this year?"

She was determined to sell me a cartridge belt. "Why don't you try one on and see how nice it feels?"

She threw the cartridge belt over my shoulder. "There," she said. "If you were wearing black silk pajamas, you'd look beautiful."

"Let me ask you something," I said. "Why do you think women have gone ape over cartridge belts?"

"What do you know what it's like to be a woman?" she asked bitterly.

148

"I didn't mean—"

"Do you think it's fun to be treated as a second-class citizen, to have to cook and sew and scrub and give birth to children?"

"No, I guess it isn't, but—"

"We're people, too," she said angrily. "And we're getting sick and tired of being sex objects."

"Please, lady," I begged.

"We've had it up to here living in a masculine society with a masculine power structure grinding us into robots. And even when we want to wear something as simple as a belt of bullets, men laugh and make fun of us."

"OK, I'll buy it. I'll buy it," I cried. "Please give me one in size twenty-two."

After the sale was made, I happened to say to the floor manager, "Boy, that's a pretty uptight salesgirl you have over there."

He just smiled and said, "That's possible, but she sells more cartridge belts than anyone else in the store."

THE SUIT THAT LOOKED
LIKE AN EDSEL

I have been looking at the new men's fashions with interest; but no matter what they tell me, I'm not going to be sucked in again. You see, I happen to be one of those unfortunate souls who was persuaded a few years back that the Nehru suit was the wave of the future.

Little did I realize that the Nehru would become to men's tailoring what the Edsel became to automobiles.

Nobody knows how many Nehru suits were actually sold during that period, mainly because very few men will admit now to having bought one. But in wardrobes all over America, attracting moths and gathering dust, hangs the stark evidence of an era that most Americans would just as soon forget.

Most of the Nehru suits sold were worn only once. The

laughter, wisecracks and snickering that greeted the wearer when he appeared in public drove him back to the dark depths of his closet, where he hid until the ridicule had subsided.

The world's record for wearing a Nehru suit is held by Robert Yoakum of Lakeville, Connecticut. Yoakum wore his suit three times—once to a college reunion, once to dinner with his in-laws and once to a Jets football game.

He was cited for bravery by the men's clothing industry, and his suit was given to the Smithsonian Institution, where it now hangs next to Lindbergh's *Spirit of St. Louis.*

Not all Nehru suit owners were as lucky. The real problem they have had is getting rid of their suits. Since most of them are new, wives have hesitated to throw them out. In cases where they have been thrown out, the trash men have refused to take them.

Goodwill Industries doesn't want them, and the Salvation Army says, "Our people may be hard up for clothes, but they have their pride."

One friend offered his Nehru suit to a hippie who told him, "You must be crazy, man. You want people to think I'm a freak?"

Another man confessed, "It wasn't a complete waste of money. My dog sleeps on it at night."

One of the problems of Nehru suit owners is that they're stuck with dozens of turtleneck sweaters and chained medallions that had to be worn with the suit.

I personally bought ten turtlenecks at the time I purchased my Nehru, because the salesman assured me I'd never have to wear a dress shirt again.

A friend of mine, who had three Nehru suits made to order for him at $200 each, tried to hang himself with one of the medallions after he realized what he'd done. But the chain on it broke, and he's now being sued by his tailor.

The question people are still asking is: Why did the Nehru fail? You can get as many answers as there are Nehru suits.

A sociologist said, "The black Nehrus for formal evening wear made men look like priests, and I think many of them became tired of always being asked to give the benediction."

And a psychiatrist said, "I think anything in America will fail that keeps a man from putting his hands in his pants pockets."

THE RUSSIANS ARE COMING

"Comrade buyers, fashion designers and state managers of state department stores. Is honor to introduce Comrade Torkel who has just completed visit to America, where he has observed new fashions now being worn on American women. Comrade Torkel."

"Is pleasure to be back in Moscow, comrades, and give report on American fashions with illustrations from magazines.

"Here, comrades, is first dress. Skirt is coming to below knees."

"But, Comrade Torkel, we've been making this dress in Leningrad dress factory for twenty years. What is new about this?"

"Am only reporting what have seen. Here second illustration. Evening pajamas to go to party in."

"You are mad, Comrade Torkel. Why would American women go to parties in their pajamas when they are richest women in world?"

"Is impossible to explain, but every reception I went to, I saw women wearing pajamas."

"But Comrade Torkel, if American women wear pajamas to party, what do they wear to bed?"

"Is nothing."

"Nothing?"

"Is called new permissiveness. Now, comrades, here is woman in pants suits."

"Are those for women railroad workers?"

"No, comrades, those are for women to go to restaurants, cocktails and dinner."

"Comrade Torkel, you are making fun of us. How can women wear pants in America when not working in factory?"

"Is being done all over."

"The Kiev Pants Cooperative has been making pants like that since the revolution."

"Is true. Now here is outfit women wear to go out shopping in. Is leather coat with leather boots and fur on collar."

"But, Comrade Torkel, this woman looks like a member of the Communist Party."

"She could be working for KGB."

"Is true. Leather coats and boots are now the fashion."

"The Gum department store in Moscow had this outfit ten years ago. We were stuck with hundreds of them."

"Next illustration. Here is peasant blouse and peasant shirt and no shoes for afternoon wear."

"But that is what they have been wearing in Smolensk since Stalin died."

"My sister, Katrina, wore an outfit like that until she got a job."

"And here, comrades, is the *pièce de résistance*. Is knickers with boots and woolen sweater and woolen hat."

"Comrade Torkel, do they have women Cossacks in America?"

"No Cossacks. Is for going to beauty parlor and nightclubs."

"To think Malinkock was sent to Siberia when his factory once tried to make knickers and they wouldn't sell."

"What are your conclusions, Comrade Torkel?"

"Is obvious, comrades, that American women want to look like Russian women. We also know Russian women all want to look the way American women *used* to look. Is possible we make barter deal. We give them all the clothes our women won't wear that we make; they give us all the clothes their women refuse to wear now."

"Comrade Torkel, is fantastic solution to our rotten-clothes problem. I am putting you in for the Lenin medal today."

9

VIRGIN POWER

SUMMER CAMPUS MAIL

Dear Mr. Altshuler,

As admissions director of Nantucket University, I am happy to inform you that you have been accepted in this fall's freshman class. Unfortunately there is some question as to whether we will open the the autumn, since the teachers and students are still on strike. I noted in your application that your father is in the pants business. I was wondering if I might prevail on you to ask him if he would be interested in hiring someone whose experience has been in the educational field but is willing to learn everything about pants. I am enclosing my résumé which I would appreciate your showing to your father at the earliest opportunity.

> Sincerely yours,
> Roger Whipthorn

Dear Vice President Agnew,

I am president of a small liberal arts college in New England, and my contract comes up for renewal in a couple of months. It is my understanding that a majority of the board are looking for a replacement for me, and I am, of course, concerned, as I feel I've done a good job.

I know how busy you are, but is there any possibility of attacking me in one of your future fund-raising speeches? An attack by you would assure me of life tenure with not only the board but the faculty as well. I am enclosing several talks I have made, underlining areas where you and I are in disagreement.

I know you have a long list of people you want to take issue with, but if you could squeeze me in in one of your attacks on the pseudo-intellectual establishment, I will be as eternally grateful as Yale's president Kingman Brewster is for all that you have done for him.

> Sincerely yours,
> Arthur Wallach

Dear Miss Collenberg,

I was sorry to receive your angry letter of June 4. I wish to point out that there was nothing personal in failing you in my Scandinavian philosophy course 5A. The fact that you called me a Swedish Fascist because I said that your midterm paper on the Chicago Seven trial was not relevant to the period we were studying did not influence my decision to give you a failing grade.

Also, I wish to assure you that the day you took off all of your clothes to protest my holding classes on Abbie Hoffman's birthday had no effect on your grades.

Even the telephone call you made to my wife telling her you were having my baby (for your information twelve students tried the same ploy) had no bearing on your F.

The only thing I judged you on was your final paper which you titled, "Hans Christian Andersen Was a Sexist Chauvinist Racist Pig," which I discovered you copied word for word from the underground newspaper *Sweat*.

Sincerely yours,
DR. SVEN KARLSON

DEAR ARNIE,
I don't know how to tell you this, but I met a boy this summer at Virginia Beach. He's a Navy fighter pilot named Brad. I guess that means that you and I won't even be able to remain good friends. But I wanted to be honest with you, Arnie. I also want to say that you don't have to pay me back the bail money I loaned you when you got busted this spring. Please don't think too unkindly of me.

Sincerely,
FRED

SUCCESS SYNDROME

I know no one will believe me, but you're just going to have to take my word for it. I met a college student the other day who said that all he wanted out of life was success and financial security.

He asked me not to use his name because he didn't want to embarrass his parents, so I shall call him Hiram.

"Hiram," I asked him, "why did you decide to take this revolutionary attitude toward society?"

"I don't know exactly when it happened. I was like most of the rest of the students. I wanted to tear down the school, the society, the establishment. I was just another conformist, and I never questioned why I was doing all the things that were expected of me.

"Then one day I thought to myself, 'There's got to be more to life than getting hit over the head by the cops.' I looked around me and saw nothing but sheep. Every student was doing his thing because someone else had done his thing, and no one was doing or saying anything new."

"So you decided to drop out of the student movement and become a millionaire?"

"Not at first. But I met this girl. She was really way out. She wore a cashmere sweater, a plaid skirt and she had on shoes and socks—I couldn't believe anyone would dress like that. But I got to talking to her, and she started making sense.

"She said it wasn't enough to lock yourself in a building or go on a hunger strike in your dorm. If you really wanted to change the world, you had to make a lot of money, and then people wouldn't tell you what to do."

"That's radical thinking," I said.

"Then she gave me a book by Professor Horatio Alger, and I guess no book I ever read has had more of an effect on me."

"Wasn't Professor Alger the one who came out first with the success-syndrome theory?"

"That's he. His story floored me. I mean, a whole new world opened for me, and I knew no matter what the consequences were and no matter what other people thought, I was going to work hard and become rich and successful. Life finally took on some meaning for me, and for the first time I felt like a free man."

"What did you do then?"

"I discovered through this girl that there were other students on campus who felt the way I did—not many, but there were enough. So we formed a group called the Students for a Successful Society. At first we had to go underground, because the administration wouldn't acknowledge us as a legitimate campus organization. But as more and more students heard about us, the SSS kept growing. We've been able to radicalize at least two hundred students who would rather be rich than do their thing."

"What are some of your activities to get more supporters?"

"We sell the *Wall Street Journal* on campus. We've opened a coffeehouse where you can read back copies of *Fortune*. We have a stock market ticker tape in the back of the room, and on weekends we have readings from the National Association of Manufacturers' Bulletins."

"Hiram, I know this all sounds great. But is it possible that this success-syndrome movement is just a passing fad?"

"No, it isn't. I know everyone calls us kooks and weirdos, but no one is going to push us around. We've already had inquiries from other campuses that want to set up similar chapters, and I wouldn't be surprised in the next few years to see what is now a minority movement become the strongest force in the country. After all, nothing succeeds like success."

THE DROPOUTS

It's become quite a fad for young folks to drop out of society and "return to the land." Everyone is very sympathetic to the people who reject the society they live in, but the big question is: How many people can a country afford to have drop out?

If everyone drops out, this is what could happen in a few years:

Myra Landon and George Coleman, two students fed up with fighting in a world they never made, decide to leave college and join friends who are working on a wheat-germ farm in Florida. But first they must rent a U-haul trailer to take their belongings. They consult the yellow pages of the phone book, call several companies listed, but get no answer.

So they get in George's battered car and drive to one of the U-haul lots. The office is padlocked. A bearded

159

fellow sitting there whittling says, "Ain't nobody there. They took off for surfing in Hawaii 'bout six months ago. Said they'd had it."

Myra and George drive to several other trailer companies but find they are also closed down. By this time their radiator is steaming, and they stop at a gas station. A man comes out and George says, "The car seems to be overheating, and we have to drive to Florida. Could you fix it?"

"Don't have anyone to fix it. Last mechanic I had went off to India to find the secret of life."

"But couldn't *you* do anything?" Myra asks.

"Don't have no spare parts," the man says. "Haven't been able to get any for fourteen months. Nobody works in the auto parts factory any more. Everyone left to do his own thing."

"Well, could you at least give us some water for the car?"

"Don't have no water. All the mains are broke, and we can't get anyone to repair them. Water company says it won't get to this area for another five months. I'll sell you a gallon of gas if you want. Have to ration it."

"A gallon of gas!" George says. "We're trying to get to Florida."

"I'd like to oblige, but we're on strict rationing since all the oil workers decided to quit and go on welfare."

"Why do you stay in business?" Myra asks.

"Got two kids living in the bottom of the Grand Canyon and I have to send them money every month or else they'd starve to death."

Myra and George start to get hungry. They walk over to a coffee shop, which is locked. So are a hamburger stand and a pizza parlor. So they find a supermarket. They walk in, and all the shelves are bare.

An old man sitting by the cash register says, "You folks looking for something?"

Myra says, "A loaf of bread?"

The man laughs. "I haven't seen a loaf of bread in months. The last bakery in the state shut down in July. All the employees took off for a rock festival in Mexico

City and never came back. Got some pickles back there if you want them. That's about the only food left. As soon as I sell them, I'm going on Social Security."

"But we haven't eaten since yesterday."

"I appreciate the problem. But we just can't get any food. You would think with all the young people going back to the farms that there would be a surplus. But they just say they want to grow enough for themselves and not make any profit for a capitalistic society."

Myra says, "It's not fair. I think the government should pass a law allowing only a certain number of people to drop out every year."

The old man says, "I couldn't agree with you more. It sure takes the fun out of dropping out when everybody decides to do it at the same time."

THE NEW LECTURE SCENE

The most popular speakers on campus these days are the student revolutionaries, black militants and those advocating the legalization of drugs.

And anyone convicted of a crime and out on bail can write his own lecture ticket.

I was at the offices of the Up Against the Wall Lecture Bureau the other day, and the phone didn't stop ringing.

"Hello, Up Against the Wall Lecture Bureau. Who's this? . . . Harvard U. What can we do for you? . . . Nope, we're sorry, the Chicago Seven are booked up through 1976. But we have some great speakers for you. How would you like Mad Dog Faucet? . . . You know, the one who wrote the book on student revolution titled *Mother Is the First to Go.*

". . . Right. Fifteen hundred dollars and expenses . . . Sure he takes off his clothes at the end . . . What kind of lecture do you think he gives? . . . Thank you. I'll send the contract. . . .

"Hello . . . What's that? You're booking speakers for Columbia U this fall? . . . Let's see . . . Here's one for you . . . Ruben Ruben . . . Yeah, that's right. He's the one who hijacked the Goodyear Blimp to Havana . . . Uh-huh. He's out on bail now . . . No, he'll be available . . . Even if he's convicted this summer he'll appeal . . . You don't think he's a draw?

"What about Abbie Satchel . . . You know, the guy who set fire to the elephant house at the Bronx Zoo during last week's anti-Vietnam demonstrations . . . He's a beautiful person . . . Two thousand bucks . . . Of course he'll get the students fired up. He spoke at Simpson Tech last week, and they burned down the library during the question period . . . Right on. He'll be there.

". . . Up Against the Wall Lecture Bureau . . . Berkeley? What can we do for you? . . . You're having a lecture series in American history and you'd like someone who is an expert in the field . . . I have just the speaker for you . . . Ziggy Rumfield . . . himself! . . . The fellow who blew off Theodore Roosevelt's nose with dynamite on Mount Rushmore . . . He's very knowledgeable about explosives . . . That's right, he shows the kids how to make a bomb right on the stage . . . No, no, the only time it ever went off was at the University of Wisconsin . . . Believe me, it's safe . . . Look, if anything happens, you don't have to pay . . . Right. Thank you."

The man hung up and I had a chance to interview him. "You seem to be really busy."

"You better believe it. Kids today want speakers they can relate to. None of this education or political baloney. They want gut speakers that will tell them how rotten it really is. Look at this. I have twenty-three requests from universities who want to hear from anyone who has killed a cop. He doesn't even have to be a big name.

"And every white school in the country wants a Black Panther to speak to them. How many Black Panthers do they think there are in this country? And look at these requests for speakers convicted of pushing drugs. I tell you, these college kids know what they want."

"At least they're interested in the world around them," I said.

"If I could get one mass murderer, I could make a fortune," he said wistfully.

162

"What other speakers are in demand at the moment?"

"Well, I can get thirty-five hundred dollars for any priest who spilled blood on draft board records. There is also a big market for the people who blew up the buildings in New York City, though I have to book them at out-of-the-way schools in case the FBI gets wind of them."

"Is there any student demand for prominent men in public life?"

"Are you kidding? Why should they listen to someone like that when they can hear from someone who has cut sugarcane in Cuba?"

AN OPENING AT THE UNIVERSITY

My friend Rory has a boy eighteen years old, who was turned down for admission by four colleges. On his fifth try he received a letter from a university asking him if he would come for an interview.

The man behind the desk asked, "How do you like the school?"

"Great. Just great."

"Do you see any way we could improve it?"

"Well, I only got here an hour ago, but I'm sure there are many ways that the school could be improved."

"I like that," the man said. "How do you get along with students?"

"Just fine, I guess. I mean, I've always gotten along with them well."

"No generation gap trouble then?"

"None that I know of."

"Do you like meeting people?"

"I suppose so. I'm an extrovert at heart."

"Do you like to entertain?"

"No, sir. I don't like to entertain at all. I keep my nose to the grindstone."

For the first time the man behind the desk seemed disappointed. "That's too bad."

Rory's son reacted immediately. "Of course, if you

want me to entertain, I'd be glad to. Heck, I used to give parties at home all the time."

"Are you any good at raising money?"

"I don't think so. I mean, I can always get a sawbuck off my old man."

"I was talking about big money," the man said.

"I can get up the tuition, if that's what you mean."

"I mean big, big money."

"Hey, what the heck kind of school is this?"

"Well," said the man behind the desk. "I believe I'd better level with you. We don't have an opening for our freshman class."

"Then what did you waste my time for?" Rory's son asked angrily as he got up.

"But we do have an opening in the school."

"As what?"

"President of the university."

"You want me to be president of the university?"

"Why not? It's a way of getting into the school. As acting president, you would get first preference from the admissions office once there was an opening in the freshman class."

"But why me?" Rory's son asked.

"We've been trying for a year to fill the job. No one will take it. Then one of the board of trustees suggested we take a freshman applicant for the university and offer him the position. The incentive would be that if he agreed to act as president, he would eventually be admitted as a student."

"I don't want to be a president," Rory's son said. "I may want to go to college, but I don't want to go that badly."

The man behind the desk was desperate. "It pays fifty thousand dollars a year. You get a house and servants and a chauffeured car."

"Forget it," Rory's son said.

"You don't have to be in at any time and you get the best seats at the football game."

"Look, if I wanted to do it, my mother and father

wouldn't let me. They want me to come back from college in one piece."

"I'm sorry you feel that way, son. From your high school record, I thought you would make a very good president."

"I may not be smart enough to get into this place as a student, but I assure you I'm not stupid enough to take a job as head of a university."

Rory's son got up and walked out. Another student walked in. As the door slowly closed, Rory's son heard the man ask the student, "How do you like the school?"

DEGREES IN MASS TRANSPORTATION

Mass transportation is definitely one of the major problems of the next decade. The ideal solution would be faster, cleaner and safer transportation for everyone. But since this is impossible, other solutions must be found to make commuting worthwhile.

Mr. Irwin Feifer, who specializes in manpower problems, has come up with an idea which certainly deserves consideration.

Feifer says that, as a commuter on the Long Island Railroad, he has been able to give hours of time to studying the transportation nightmare of the seventies.

On the basis of his own experience he has applied a system-analysis approach to commuting which, when boiled down to layman's language, can be put this way: "How can time now used to look at your watch be otherwise employed constructively and productively to further the welfare of the country?"

The Feifer Plan is to incorporate all railroads as universities and allow commuters to take courses for bona fide college or graduate credits.

While the Long Island and Penn Central trains slowly made their way toward their destinations, each car would become a classroom where commuters could do their lessons, listen to guest lectures by experts who are stuck on the trains, and be graded by the conductors who punched their tickets.

A delay would no longer mean an inconvenience but would actually be credited to the student as an hour or two hours of classroom work.

In order not to confuse the courses, each car would specialize in a different field of study and would be so marked on the outside. When buying your ticket at the gate, you would specify what subject you would like to take for the month, and the agent would issue you books at the same time he sold you a ticket.

The Feifer Plan is not without incentives and subsidies. One of the major provisions of the plan is to get a grant from the federal office of education which would be used as an inducement for commuters to take the courses.

Each month a true-or-false test would be given by the conductor. Those who received 90 or over would be granted a $5.50 reduction on their commuter tickets for the following months. Those scoring 80 or above would get a $3.25 reduction, and those who passed with a 65 would not be given a money reduction but would be assured a seat on the train for the next four weeks.

The Feifer Plan is not necessarily aimed just at people who take railroads (a subway educational plan where people can study while being delayed in tunnels is now being worked out), but could also be applied to people driving to work in the morning.

Those signing up for credits would listen to lectures on the radio in the morning and evening rush hours and do their book studying at traffic bottlenecks and red lights.

The driver students would hand in their tests at toll booths, and the toll collectors would grade them as they made change.

Most people would not mind traffic delays, as it would give them more time to get their homework done.

The Feifer Plan would provide for graduation exercises every six months. In the case of the railroads, the ceremonies would be held at the railroad stations with the Secretary of Transportation handing out the diplomas.

Automobile college graduates would receive their diplomas from the license bureau, and each license plate would indicate how many degrees the driver possessed.

The plan, if put into effect, would make Americans the most educated people in the world. It would also turn train delays and traffic jams into a profit. But more important, with everyone going to school, the generation gap could become a thing of the past.

THE BLACK BRAIN-DRAIN

One of the reasons President Nixon's Black Capitalism Program has been a bust is that there is a black brain-drain in this country, and it's getting more serious all the time.

A black businessman told me the other day that every time he trains somebody in his organization, a white company comes along and hires him away.

"All that black businesses are doing these days is training black people so they can be grabbed by white employers, who are willing to pay anything to get a qualified black in the organization.

"A few months ago, I sent my advertising manager over to a magazine to discuss a campaign. He never came back. The magazine people hired him on the spot.

"Every time a white person comes to the office to discuss business with me, he walks out with one of my secretaries.

"I've had girls come in here typing fifteen words a minute at the start. I patiently put up with their mistakes and their speed and their confusion until finally they were up to sixty words a minute. As soon as they hit their stride, they're kidnapped by Xerox or IBM or AT&T, and I have to start all over with a fifteen-word-a-minute apprentice."

"You got problems," I told him.

"I'm afraid to send my people out to see customers, and I'm afraid to let my customers come to my office. It's a helluva way to run a business."

The businessman told me he wasn't the only one feeling

the black brain-drain. "I have a black friend in the franchise business. He was prevailed upon to open a drive-in restaurant. They told him they would give him all the money and help he needed. But every time he gets somebody good, the franchise company makes the black trainee an assistant manager and puts him in charge of another restaurant. My friend feels like he's running a restaurant school.

"I have another friend who has a black law firm. He's afraid to send one of his younger lawyers out to argue a case with a white law office because he knows they'll offer the black lawyer a partnership in the firm. How is black capitalism supposed to work if they keep swiping all our skilled people from us?"

"I guess President Nixon didn't think of that," I said.

"They're not just doing it in businesses. They're stealing all the good black professors from black colleges and universities, too. Every time a white school hears about a good black professor at a black school, they offer him twice his salary and the chairmanship of a department.

"This backfired, though, at Howard University last year. Some Midwest school was looking for a black professor for its science department, so it called Howard University and asked them if they had a man they could spare. They didn't specify race, assuming he would be black. Howard suggested a man. The Midwest school official hired the person, sight unseen. But when he showed up for the term, they were flabbergasted to find that they had hired another white professor."

"What do you think the administration should do about it?"

"Well, if our only role in business is to train black people for white companies, then we think the white companies and the government should pay us for it. Rather than call ourselves companies, we'll call ourselves labor consultants. Then when we send someone out on a call, we won't be so nervous if he doesn't come back."

RECRUITING BLACK SCHOLARS

There was a time when the major preoccupation of our nation's universities was recruiting athletes for their football and basketball teams. But all this has changed. Now the big recruiting drive among our schools is to find qualified black students for their scholastic programs.

Every university president knows his school is no longer judged by any other standard than how many black students are enrolled in the school.

Alumni have been alerted to immediately report on any outstanding black scholar, and alumni clubs have been set up to get around the strict "black student scholastic-recruiting code."

It's hard to keep your head if you're a high school student and you're suddenly in demand.

Take the case of Bernard Jefferson Smith, a straight-A black student at Central High School in Maple County, Pennsylvania. Reports about Bernard's scholastic achievements started leaking out in his sophomore year, and scouts from every major university in the country started sneaking in the back of Bernard's math classes to see if he was as good as they said he was.

What they saw amazed them. Bernard was even better at geometry and calculus than his press notices indicated.

According to the "black student scholastic-recruiting code," scouts are not permitted to approach a black student about a scholarship until he is in his senior year. But this didn't stop eager alumni from making approaches on their own.

One day, during his junior year, Bernard found a brand-new Corvette in his driveway with a note on it. The unsigned note said: "MIT has the best Biochemistry Department in the country."

A few weeks later, the paid-up mortgage on his parents' house arrived in an unmarked envelope which had just two words on the top: "Think Stanford."

Not long after that, work started on a swimming pool

in Bernard's yard. When Bernard inquired as to who was paying for it, the contractor said, "I have no idea. We were told to send the bill to the Harvard Club in Philadelphia."

Bernard's father, who worked as a porter at the local bank, was suddenly and mysteriously made a vice-president. The president of the bank, a University of Pennsylvania graduate, told Bernard's father the promotion was long overdue and invited him and Bernard to have dinner with the dean of Penn's Wharton School of Business Administration.

But the pressure really didn't start until Bernard began his senior year. There were so many university chancellors camped on Bernard's doorstep every night that he had to sneak in the house disguised as a welfare worker.

The telephone never stopped ringing.

Numbered Swiss bank accounts were opened in Bernard's name.

A wealthy alumnus at Yale said he would build a new library and name it the Bernard Jefferson Smith Building if Bernard would go to New Haven.

Finally, as Bernard was still trying to make up his mind, the phone rang. The voice on the other end said, "Bernard, this is the President of the United States, Richard Nixon. Have you ever thought of going to Whittier College?"

VIRGIN POWER

There have been so many groups formed lately to protect their sexual freedoms that little attention has been given to a new activist organization called the Virgin Anti-Defamation League.

The organization was started a few years ago by a small group of people who were sick and tired of virgins being the butt of every joke, every salacious comedy and every tired sexual cliché.

Sidney Pimpledown, the president of VADL, told me the response to the organization has been heartwarming. New chapters are springing up all over the country.

Pimpledown said, "We estimate that there are approximately 1,980,543 virgins in the United States at the present, including at least 1,200 women. These people have been led to believe that there is some sort of shame attached to being a virgin. We want virtuous people to be proud of their heritage. We point out that some of our greatest writers, poets and artists have been virgins. Even today, in some primitive culture, there is a premium placed on virtue."

"Then one of your goals," I said, "is to bring virginity out in the open and get people to accept it for what it is?"

"That's correct. Until recently it was a dark secret one kept to himself. The majority of virgins refused to talk about it even to each other. But now, thanks to VADL, virgins know they are not alone, that there are almost two million people in the same boat with them. They are good people: Priests, college students, university professors, naval officers and even Avon ladies."

"Our job," Pimpledown continued, "is to convince them they are not the monsters society has made them out to be."

"What do you do besides make virgins feel they are not alone?"

"We have been lobbying for equal treatment for virgins. Do you realize a virtuous secretary makes twenty percent less salary than any other kind of secretary? Virgins are discriminated against in bars, at parties and even drive-in theaters."

"We also," continued Pimpledown, "are demanding the employment of more virgins on television commercials. In the past, cast directors for TV commercials refused to hire virgins, as they were afraid the local TV stations would object, but when we proved to them that virgins were as good at performing on TV as anybody else, they changed their policy. It took time, but now all major advertisers include two virgins in their budgets."

"That is a breakthrough," I said.

"Our main function is education," Pimpledown said. "We go on television and give our side of the story. For years the talk shows refused to book virgins on their pro-

171

grams. But there is a more enlightened view now. We even had a virgin on the Johnny Carson show last week, and they only received a hundred and fifty protest calls. Three years ago, if Carson had interviewed a virgin, the whole board would have lit up."

"You've come a long way," I told Pimpledown.

"We're starting to fight back. The militant arm of our organization is called Virgin Power. We've picketed movies with the word 'virgin' in the title. We've burned pornographic books that show virgins as weak, cringing people. And we've held sit-ins at city halls demanding virgins be permitted to get married."

"Mr. Pimpledown, what do you consider your biggest success so far?"

"Without doubt," he said, "the biggest success we've had so far was getting the Department of Interior to stop referring to Alaska as 'virgin territory.'"

10

HOW THEY MERGED SANTA CLAUS

NOBODY PAYS

Everyone has his own theory as to why the economy is in such trouble. In spite of all the gobbledygook the administration is putting out, the real reason the economy has gone to pot is that nobody is paying his bills.

My father, who is president, vice-president, treasurer and sole full-time employee of the Aetna Curtain Company, in New York City, called me in Washington to tell me what was going on in the business world.

"If that President of *yours* really wants to get the economy moving again," he said, "you can tell him to get people to start paying their bills."

"You mean people aren't paying their bills?" I said, astonished.

"No one is paying bills. People, companies, corporations, banks, insurance companies. Everyone is holding up on the money."

"It's hard to believe."

"Believe it," my father said. "I made curtains for a toy company's showroom on Fifth Avenue three months ago. They still haven't paid me. I went over the other day and said, 'Look, you're a big toy company; I'm a small manufacturer. Why don't you pay me for the curtains?' They said, 'We'd love to pay you for the curtains but Krum's Department Store hasn't paid us for our toys.'

"So," my father continued, "I went over to Krum's Department Store and said to them, 'Why don't you pay the Thumbsucker Toy Company for their toys so they can pay me for my curtains?' The people at Krum's Department Store said, 'We'd love to pay the Thumbsucker Company for their toys, but none of our charge accounts has paid us. Here is a customer, Arthur Gordon. He bought a hundred dollars worth of toys and he hasn't paid for them.' "

My father went to see Arthur Gordon and said, "Mr. Gordon, I don't know you, but you owe the Krum Department Store a hundred dollars."

"What business is it of yours?" Mr. Gordon wanted to know.

"Because if you don't pay your bill, the Krum people won't pay the Thumbsucker Toy Company, and if they don't get paid, they won't pay me for my curtains."

"Well," said Gordon, "if you must know, I'm a lawyer, and I won't pay Krum's until Harold Jaffe, who is in the lumber business, pays me."

My father went to see Jaffe, who said, "The reason I haven't paid Gordon is that the Man Mountain Construction Company owes me five thousand dollars for lumber. You get my five thousand dollars from Man Mountain and I'll pay my lawyer's bill."

Since business was slow, my father went to see the Man Mountain Construction Company. They admitted owing Jaffe the money, but said the reason they couldn't pay him was that the Third National Bank of Queens Village had refused to give Man Mountain a loan to finish a housing project they were building in Happy Valley, New York.

My father went to see Mr. Michael Kahme, president of the Third National Bank of Queens Village, and he said the reason they couldn't lend Man Mountain any money was because a dentist named Dr. Hiram Torem hadn't paid back a loan he made to furnish his office with all-new dental equipment.

Dr. Torem told my father he couldn't pay back the loan for his equipment because Mr. Robert Cantor hadn't paid him for a very expensive set of false teeth.

My father told me, "I knew it was hopeless to look up Mr. Cantor, so I went back to the shop where I found Mr. Sam Plotnik, who sold me the fabric for the curtains I made for the Thumbsucker Toy Company. He said, 'When am I going to get the money for my curtain material?' I said to him, 'What's the hurry?' And he said, 'The hurry is that I've had to lay off people because you haven't paid your bill.'"

And my father said, "One of those people wouldn't be named Robert Cantor, would he?"

"No," said Plotnik. "Why do you ask?"

My father replied, "It was just a hunch."

WHERE HAVE ALL THE TIPSTERS GONE?

You used to meet them everywhere—at cocktail parties, dinners, the beach club and college reunions.

Although they came in all shapes and forms, they had one thing in common. They were the people who had invested in Xerox when it was $9 a share, Litton Industries when it was $10, and Gulf & Western when it was $14. They used to tell you how they had first heard about Texas Instruments when it was selling for a song, how they had gotten into Ling-Temco-Vought through a fraternity brother; and how they had bought Penn Central, Computer Data, Fairchild Camera against the advice of their brokers.

They weren't unfriendly people. They always had time to chat with you and tell you how well they were doing in the market. They implied that they had a sixth sense about investing in Wall Street and a talent for these matters that you, the average person, would never understand.

Without intending to do it, they made you feel completely inadequate as a breadwinner and a sucker for holding onto a salaried job.

But in the last few months something has happened to these people. For one thing, you hardly see them anymore, and when you do, they're very quiet. Their clothes have gotten seedy—the bounce has gone from their walk—and when they hold a drink, their hands shake a lot.

I ran into one the other day on a plane. His name was Simpkin. The last time we flew up to New York, a few years ago, Simpkin was dropping names like Planet Oil, M-G-M and Boeing Aircraft.

This time I hardly recognized him when I sat down. His hair was completely white, his eyes were bloodshot, and he had a tic in his right cheek.

"How are things going?" I asked pleasantly.

"This seat is taken," he snarled.

"It's me, Simpkin. You know, from the Washington Athletic Club. Remember when we had that nice talk about American Nursing Homes merging with Rorshach Matches? Whatever happened to that?"

"If you say one more word to me, I'll hit you in the mouth," he said.

"Good heavens, Simpkin, you're overwrought. Are you still in the market?"

He raised his fist, but the stewardess came by and asked him to fasten his safety belt. Simpkin wiped his brow. "I'm sorry," he said, "but National General is down to two and one-half."

"Oh," I said. "I didn't know. Were you big in National General?"

"Not as big as I was in Commonwealth United and Chrysler."

"I don't follow the market," I said. "But I understand there have been some reverses. Would this be a good time to buy anything?"

"As soon as the FASTEN YOUR BELT sign goes off," Simpkin said, "I'm going to kill you."

"Grab hold of yourself, man," I cried. "After all, money isn't everything."

"Do you know how much I was *once* worth on paper?" Simpkin said.

"A lot, I'm sure."

"Would you believe seven hundred and fifty thousand dollars?"

I whistled. "I would have never known it."

"Do you know what I'm worth on paper now?"

"I won't guess."

"I owe fifty thousand, and they're still asking for margin."

"You don't look it," I replied.

"You s.o.b.," Simpkin yelled, "you probably had your money in a savings and loan bank all this time."

"As a matter of fact, I did. And you know something, Simpkin? When I opened the account, they gave my wife a thirty-six-piece set of Pyroware dishes."

Simpkin cried all the rest of the way to New York.

INFLATION AND THE GOOD GUYS

Since everyone seems to be interested in what will happen to the economy of the United States in the seventies, I invited a distinguished panel of the nation's leading businessmen, labor leaders, economists and government forecasters to a meeting in Washington, D.C., to discuss the subject. The meeting was held in the shadow of the White House: in a booth at a Walgreen's Drugstore, to be exact.

Here are some excerpts from the discussion:

Elias Endicott of the Banking Institute of Compounded Quarterly Interest was very optimistic: "The challenge of the seventies will be closely tied to the monetary policies of the government. If Washington gives the banks permission to raise the rates of interest on money borrowed, to a reasonable eighteen and one-third percent, and at the same time permits us to pay no more than two and an eighth percent interest on money deposited by our clients, we could send the inflationary spiral into a downtrend by 1975."

Sheldon Carbon, president of the Recall Motor Company, believes the key to the fight against inflation is labor's attitude toward wage increases. "Labor must be responsible and realize that any demands for wage increases will only heat up the economy.

"No one is more sympathetic to the rise of the cost of living of the average worker than management. At the same time, labor is only hurting itself when it makes unreasonable wage demands at a time when everyone should tighten his belt. To show that Recall Motors is serious about wanting to keep inflation from getting out of hand, the Recall board of directors has voted to increase the price of their new 1971 models by only $891.50, which still makes a two-door, four-cylinder Recall at $10,980 one of the best buys in the country."

Rock Sloboda, president of the United Typewriter, Sandstone, Match and Picture-Framing Federation of Labor, felt that the seventies would be an opportunity for everyone to show good faith. "We want to keep our demands in the ball park," Sloboda told the panel. "Therefore we will not ask for a three-hour, four-day week, with double time for coffee breaks. We will stick to the same demands we made last year: a four-hour, three-day week, with a two-month paid vacation every year. If management agrees to what we believe is the absolute minimum our members will accept, we see no reason for industry to increase its prices in the next ten years."

Alexander Bell XII, the telephone company's vice-president in charge of public relations, said the phone company was working on more efficient and cheaper phone service than the American public had ever had before. To provide this cheaper service, the phone company was asking for an increase in rates for the early seventies of only 33⅓ percent.

Charles Fairweather, President Nixon's adviser on inflationary trends, said the administration still felt the solution to inflation was a "full-unemployment program."

"Without belaboring the point," he told the panel, "the basic reason for inflation is that people have too much money to spend. If they are not working, the problem of inflation will take care of itself."

While the panel members came to no hard conclusions, they all agreed that the causes of inflation were other irresponsible forces at work in the country, who, unlike him, did not have the best interests of the United States at heart.

A NATION OF BANKS

Every time an old building is torn down in this country, and a new building goes up, the ground floor becomes a bank.

The reason for this is that banks are the only ones who can afford the rent for the ground floor of the new buildings going up. Besides, when a bank loans someone money to build a new building, it usually takes an option for the street-floor facilities.

Most people don't think there is anything wrong with

this, and they accept it as part of the American free-enterprise system. But there is a small group of people in this country who are fighting for Bank Birth Control.

This is how Huddlestone Hubbard, the BBC's chairman, explained it:

"Whenever you see an old building torn down," Hubbard said, "you usually see a candy store, a dry cleaner, a delicatessen and possibly a florist torn down with it. These shops are all replaced in the new building with a beautiful glass, aluminum, wall-to-wall-carpeted money factory.

"Now from an aesthetic viewpoint, a bank looks better than a dry cleaner, a candy store, a delicatessen and a florist. But from a practical point of view, it's a sheer disaster. If you want a newspaper, a candy bar or a chocolate milk shake, you can't get it at a bank. Nor can you run out to a bank for a pound of Swiss cheese and a six-pack of beer when you have guests coming over.

"A bank is great if you want to buy a car, but it's useless if you want to have your dress cleaned.

"And while a bank might buy flowers to give itself a human image, it doesn't sell any when you want to make up with your wife."

"What you're saying then, Mr. Hubbard, is that every time a bank goes up, something in all of us dies."

"Exactly. One of the reasons kids are getting in so much trouble these days is that there are no candy stores to hang around anymore. When they tear down a delicatessen, the tangy smells of potato salad, salamis, corned beef and dill pickles are lost forever. Unless you're trying to make a loan, no one ever salivates in a bank."

"It's true," I said.

"The situation is more crucial than anyone thinks," Hubbard said. "At the rate they're tearing down consumer stores and replacing them with banks, we estimate that in ten years it will be impossible to buy a loaf of bread in the country. What good is it to get seven percent on your money if you starve to death?"

"Then what you're saying is that it isn't a question of not taking it with you. It's a question of staying alive while you have it," I said.

180

"Something like that," Hubbard agreed. "We're trying to get the public to wake up to the fact that it's better to have a store that sells screwdrivers than a bank that gives away alarm clocks."

"What's the solution?"

"A government decree that a bank has to supply the same services of the stores it tore down on the same property. If it's a bakery, they have to sell cake; if it's a photography shop, they have to develop film; and if it's a dry-goods store, they have to sell warm underwear. If they provide the services of the store they tore down, then we'll let them do a little moneylending on the side."

HINTS FOR TAX TIME

One of the paradoxes of the American tax system is that it's easier for a man to deduct a strange lady from a business trip than it is to deduct his own wife. The IRS authorities will believe that a strange lady could easily be of value to a businessman in the capacity of a secretary, or what have you, but they're very skeptical that a wife could serve any useful function.

Not long ago, the Research Institute of America put out a helpful guide for husbands wanting to deduct their wives from business trips they took together.

Here are some of the suggestions made. The examples are mine.

(1.) During a trip, keep a record of all the services your wife performed that could be described as *necessary* rather than merely *helpful*. One test: If your wife stayed home, would you have needed to bring someone else along?

Example: Mrs. Plumbell's justification: "My husband, George Plumbell, would never have made it without bringing me along. If I hadn't been in the room to receive the long-distance call from California, I wouldn't have been able to get George off the golf course, and he might have lost the Worthington Crushed Papaya account. George's friends and associates told me many times dur-

181

ing the convention that if I hadn't come along, he would have certainly brought someone else with him."

(2.) If possible, show what business resulted from your wife having accompanied you, for "nothing succeeds like success."

Example: "If it hadn't been for my wife, Myra, I would never have been able to unload those faulty mussel valves on the Bureau of Off-Limits Drilling. The purchasing agent was so busy pinching my wife under the table that he signed the order without reading the specifications. Myra was black and blue for a week."

(3.) Keep any letters from customers received before or after a business trip showing that your wife's presence was desired or appreciated.

Example: "Dear Archie: It was great seeing Priscilla at the knife sharpeners' convention last week. She was really a sight for sore eyes, and when she danced on the table, topless, at three o'clock in the morning, she *made* the convention. All the wives are still talking about it.

"I also want to tell you how much we enjoyed the snake dance she led through the Hilton Hotel in the early hours of the morning.

"Here is your share of the damage. We prorated it between Priscilla, Marge Bernheim and Hilda Marton who seemed to have the best time of all the women. I hope you'll bring Priscilla next year. People are already inquiring if she'll be there."

(4.) Photographs of your wife with customers or other business associates (and of course their wives) may be helpful, as well as shots of her at their factories or other places of business.

Example: "Dear Sir: Enclosed please find a selection of photos taken at our medical convention which I am enclosing with my tax return. The lady dealing the cards at our cabana in Nassau is my wife. The other three gin players are Mrs. Selma Rosenkrantz, wife of the vice-president of the Do or Die Surgical Supply Company, Mrs. Frederick Piltdown, whose husband is president of the First National Blood Bank of Terre Haute, and Mrs.

Jennifer Cook, wife of the executive director of Medicare Transplant Mutual Fund.

"The second photo is of my wife visiting the first-aid room at the Paradise Island Gambling Casino, and the third photo shows her swimming in the ocean with some of the leading neurosurgeons from all over the country."

These are only a few of the tips that are offered to justify your wife going with you on a business trip. If you find it too much bother, the best thing to do is leave your wife at home and take someone with you whom the Internal Revenue people trust.

FIGHTING INFLATION

The wonderful thing about American industry is that it rises to every challenge. Even something as distasteful as inflation has not discouraged most manufacturers. Their solution to the problem is not in the product but in the package. Rather than raise the prices on many goods, American industry is devising new methods to make the product smaller, while making the package larger. In this way, the customer feels assured that nothing has changed.

I visited one of the largest packaging companies in the country the other day to see how they were doing it. The vice-president in charge of inflationary design took me around the plant.

"We're going twenty-four hours a day," he said proudly. "Everyone is asking us for new designs to help them get through this rough period."

I noticed women in white smocks working with tweezers under microscopes.

"What are those women doing?" I asked.

"Those are five-cent chocolate bars on their tweezers. They put each one in that large aluminum foil and then they wrap wax paper around it. Over the wax paper they put the name of the chocolate bar in large letters. Here's one that's finished."

"Why from the outside it looks like an old-fashioned chocolate bar!"

"No one can tell the difference until they open the package," he said proudly.

We went into another part of the building. There were air hoses hanging all over the ceiling and boxes were rolling along a conveyor belt.

I looked perplexed.

"We're packaging soap flakes in here," he shouted above the din. "The lady down at the beginning of the line puts one teaspoonful of soap flakes into those giant-sized boxes; then those men over there with the hoses pump air into the rest of the box."

"How ingenious!" I shouted back.

"The bottom of the box is weighted with very heavy cardboard so no one will know, when picking up the box, how much soap flakes there are in it."

"That's a lot of air to put in a box."

"We don't use the air for only soap flakes. We also use it for cereals, baking products and anything that comes in a box.

"Let me show you this invention which we have a patent on. This is a see-through wax paper window for noodles. Well, when you look at it, you think you're getting a full box of noodles. Right?"

"Of course."

"Now, look at the inside of the box."

"Why, the only noodles in it are stuck to the window," I said in amazement.

"Yep. The windows and the noodles are magnetized. When the window fills up with noodles, the box moves on."

"Are those frozen TV dinners over there?"

"They certainly are. They look like a complete dinner, don't they?"

"You bet."

"Now, look under the tray. You see how it's indented. There's nothing in the tray but what you see on the top."

"Fantastic," I said.

He took me into another building which had a large sign, PHARMACEUTICALS, on the outside. "This is where we work on new packaging for medicines." He opened a door, and everywhere I looked were large mounds of white cotton.

"What do you do with that stuff?" I asked.

"We put two pills in each bottle of medicine and stuff the rest of it with white cotton. If it wasn't for cotton, I don't think the drug industry could survive."

"You people think of everything."

"Not everything. Our dream is to devise a package filled with nothing but air, cotton and aluminum foil. If you bought one, you'd get a second package free."

FREE GIFTS FOR ALL

The nation's savings banks have gone into the free gift business in a big way. In order to attract depositors, the banks are giving away everything from color TV sets to lawn mowers, and the competition to give away gifts is getting fierce.

I went into a bank the other day to break a twenty-dollar bill, and as I arrived at the window, the cashier handed me a pressure cooker.

"No," I said, "I don't want a pressure cooker, I just want to—"

She leaned down and came up with a box. "How about a steam iron with twenty-one steam vents?"

"Thank you very much, but I would like to—"

"All right. We'll give you a clock radio that lights up in the dark."

"Miss, I don't want to be ungrateful, but all I need is change for a twenty-dollar bill."

The cashier pressed a button, and suddenly two bank guards were standing on each side of me. "Come this way please and don't make a fuss."

They escorted me to the desk of a vice-president and stood on each side of me, their hands on their revolvers.

"Doesn't want the pressure cooker, the steam iron or the clock radio," one of the guards said.

"A real troublemaker," the other guard added.

The vice-president said, "I'm sure we can work something out."

"Good," I said, handing him the twenty-dollar bill.

"Put your money away," he said angrily. Then he took out a catalog. "Would you settle for a three-piece bedroom set?"

I shook my head.

"All right, we'll put in a new kitchen for you, but you'll have to keep the twenty dollars in for a full year."

"I don't want to deposit the twenty dollars. I just want change for it."

The vice-president looked at me quizzically.

"Keep an eye on him," he said to the guards. Then he disappeared into an inner office. He returned fifteen minutes later with another man who introduced himself as a senior vice-president. "I see Collins here has been offering you a lot of junk. It's obvious you're a man of taste and elegance."

"Thank you," I said. I held up the twenty-dollar bill.

"Come this way," the senior vice-president said, taking my twenty-dollar bill.

He ushered me into his office which was covered with paintings. "Now we can either give you this original El Greco, or the Van Gogh, providing you don't withdraw the twenty dollars in the bank for two years."

"They're very nice, but I need the money."

"You are difficult, aren't you? Would you consider a quarter interest in the Pan Am Building? For that you would have to leave the twenty dollars in for five years."

I was getting angry. "Look," I said, "I do not wish to open an account in your bank. If you don't want to change my twenty-dollar bill, I'll go across the street."

"All right, if you're going to be tough, we'll get tough," he said. "We'll give you a private plane, a Rolls-Royce, and Bebe Rebozo's home in Key Biscayne, Florida. That's our final offer."

I took the twenty dollars back in disgust and went across the street to the other bank. But I was blocked at the door by four FBI agents.

"What's going on?" I asked.

186

"There's been a holdup," one of the FBI men said. "The robbers got away with three phonographs, a garbage disposal unit and an electric blanket."

HOW THEY MERGED SANTA CLAUS

Although there was a great deal of excitement at the time of the merger of Santa Claus and the conglomerate of Consolidated Consortium United, it did not work out as well as everyone had expected.

If you recall, a press conference was held at the North Pole, where Harley B. Dickens, the chairman of the board of Consolidated, announced that his company had bought out Santa Claus for $150,000,000 worth of Consolidated stock, which was then selling at $14 a share.

Mr. Claus was reluctant to sell the operation, but his wife had insisted. "You're getting old and you have to think about your security when you stop working," she said.

Dickens told the press there would be absolutely no change in the Santa Claus operation, and it would continue as it had in the past. Santa Claus would still be in charge, and the only thing that CCU would contribute would be top-flight management, resources and efficiency. Dickens pointed out that since CCU was a worldwide company, more children would benefit from Christmas than ever before.

"We are not changing the image of Santa Claus," he said. "We'll just be streamlining it."

After pictures were taken of Mr. Claus and Mr. Dickens, the chairman returned to New York and for several months Santa Claus continued to operate as he had done in the past.

But one day a CCU systems-analysis expert reported to Dickens that he made a study of the Santa Claus setup and he had several suggestions as to how to improve it.

"The idea of children writing individual letters to Santa Claus is time-consuming and wasteful. It takes ten elves working eight hours a day to open and read all the mail.

187

This is wasteful and inefficient and requires overtime to fill all the orders.

"I therefore suggest that we make all children write to Santa Claus on computer cards, checking off the toys they want. We would put a warning on the cards that any child who bends, folds or mutilates a card would be automatically cut off Santa's list."

Dickens okayed the idea, and although Santa Claus protested vigorously that it would take the personal touch out of Christmas, the chairman assured him that Consolidated would run a large advertising campaign explaining that the computer card would actually make writing to Santa more fun.

A computer complex was installed at the North Pole, and several gnomes were hired to feed it.

Unfortunately, a few months later, while Santa Claus and his elves were hard at work, the Consolidated stock started slipping. From $14 a share, it went down to $10. Dickens ordered economies. First, he depleted the work force in Santa's toy shop by 50 percent. Then, instead of a list of 100 toys for children to choose from, he cut it down to 3.

He announced "regretfully" that because of the state of the economy, there would have to be a handling charge on every parcel delivered more than 30 miles from the North Pole.

Once again, Santa protested, but to no avail. The Consolidated stock was now selling at $2 a share, and Dickens telexed Mr. Claus, "Get rid of the reindeer."

This was too much for Santa Claus, and he took his life savings, $2,500, and offered to buy back his own company. By then Consolidated had filed for bankruptcy, and the creditors were happy to take anything they could get.

"We were millionaires on paper," Santa said to his wife as he put the last touches on a doll house. "But I stopped believing in myself."

"I was wrong, Santa," Mrs. Claus said tearfully. "Better you should work for yourself and die with your boots on."

The first thing Santa Claus did before making his deliveries on Christmas was to load the computer on his sleigh and drop it on Harley Dickens' home.

BEFORE THE AX FALLS

As the earnings statements of large companies get gloomier there is more and more pressure on corporation executives to make economies in their firms. Most companies do this first by firing the office boy, then retrenching in the mail room department, and finally cutting the budget on the softball team.

But as time goes on and stockholders get unhappier and unhappier, management may have to start making cuts in the upper levels of the company, and even executives are in danger of losing their jobs.

How does someone in a large company save his job when all around him are losing theirs? Perhaps I can be of help.

The first bit of advice is DO NOT TAKE A VACATION this year. No matter how badly you need one, hang in there, or else this is what could happen:

"Maxwell, what are you doing sitting at my desk?"

"Oh, Herndon, how was the Cape?"

"Fine. Now what are you doing in my office?"

"Well, finance decided to merge sales with packaging, and they asked me to take over. I naturally fought the move, but they were adamant. We tried to reach you on the Cape, but they said you were racing in the Hyannis-Nantucket sailboat trials. How did you do?"

"I came in third. Now where have I been moved to?"

"That's what they were trying to reach you about. They've had to cut across the board. I spoke up for you but. . . ."

The second bit of advice is to institute an economy committee, before one is constituted without you. Go into the president and say, "B. J., I'd like to organize a cost-cutting program so we don't get caught like Penn Central with our pants down. What I suggest we do is form a team and go into every department and see how we can eliminate waste. We could report to you within a month, so you'll have something to show the board."

If your idea is accepted, you must use great tact in suggesting the elimination of somebody else's job, on the off chance that he might survive and do you in.

You could say, "Gentlemen, I think we'd make a mistake if we let Fowler go. It's true his advertising campaign for Fluff was a complete disaster, but we must remember there has been great consumer resistance in toiletries for dogs this year. Fowler is a genius when it comes to advertising, even though he has a tendency to antagonize everyone in the company."

If Fowler loses his job, you have the minutes of the meeting to prove that you've defended him.

To show that you have the company's interest at heart before your own, announce some economies you're making in your own department. "I'm happy to announce, gentlemen, that I've furloughed two telephone operators and laid off four watchmen in our Wichita warehouse, thus saving the company thirty-three thousand dollars. This cuts my department to the bone, but I believe we can manage with what we've got."

The biggest danger during an economy drive is that the company may hire an outside consulting firm to make a private report on which people should be let go.

If one comes in the plant, *stop all work you are doing* and spend every waking moment with him. Most consultants know little or nothing about the businesses they are investigating, and if you can make them look good, they may believe you are necessary to the firm.

You can also get even with some old enemies.

"Tell me, Herndon, where is Mr. Maxwell?"

"Maxwell? I believe he's playing golf. He always plays golf on Wednesday afternoon with his doctor."

CANCELING INSURANCE

There has been a rash of automobile insurance cancellations lately by the major companies, and everyone is very nervous about it. The other day my wife was notified that her auto insurance policy was being canceled. The notification gave no reason for the cancellation, and since my wife had not been in an accident or had ever made a claim, she was perplexed.

She asked me to get to the root of it, and I took the next plane to visit our insurance company. The company is housed in a 56-story aluminum and tinted-glass skyscraper on a 30-acre shopping plaza overlooking most of the state of Connecticut.

I arrived on the 35th floor where one made inquiries concerning canceled insurance policies. After browsing through the company literature, which told how insurance was making America great, I was ushered into the office of Clyde Featherstone.

I gave Mr. Featherstone the cancellation notice, and he clucked once or twice and then disappeared. He returned in a few moments with the folder.

"What did my wife do wrong?" I demanded.

"Your wife didn't do anything wrong. Her records are all up to snuff."

"Then why did you cancel her insurance?"

"Because of Trembling and Trembling, her insurance agents."

"Trembling and Trembling?" I said.

"Yes," said Featherstone, going through the folder. "They've been very naughty boys, very naughty indeed."

"Did they steal any money?" I asked.

"Worse! They've written too many policies this year that people have made claims on. We've had to pay out $1,897 to Trembling and Trembling clients in the last twelve months."

"But what's that got to do with my wife's insurance policy? She didn't get any of the money."

"Ah, but since you are with Trembling and Trembling, *you* are now considered a bad risk. Their record is your record."

"That's nonsense. I hardly know Trembling and Trembling," I protested. "I wouldn't recognize them if I saw them on the street. This is guilt by association."

Featherstone smiled. "You came to us through Trembling and Trembling, and you will leave with Trembling and Trembling. This company will not put up with people who make insurance claims against it."

"But that's what you're here for," I said. "To pay people off when something happens."

"That's a foul lie," said Featherstone, losing his smile. "We're here to build buildings and real-estate developments, and finance ships and airplanes and ball parks. If we keep paying out claims, where would we get the money to construct this fifty-six-story building, with its beautiful shopping plaza and underground computer center?

"Do you realize," said Featherstone, "that every dollar we pay out in a claim is a dollar we have to take away from our advertising budget, which tells the public what wonderful insurance people we are?"

"I appreciate all that," I said, "but surely you have to pay some claims in order to stay in the insurance business."

"That's what Trembling and Trembling thought," Featherstone said as he tore up my wife's folder.

I thanked Featherstone for his kindness and understanding. He got up to shake my hand. "If you're staying in town for dinner, we have a great restaurant on the roof garden which is bringing us fifteen-percent profit a year."

GOOD-BYE, JONES

The big question on everybody's mind in 1971 is: What happened to the economy and where did we go wrong? It's easy to blame the Nixon administration for the economic slowdown, but, if the truth be known, Nixon had nothing to do with it.

The trouble started with a man named Harry Putnam, who lived on Maple Street, next to a man named Robert Jones.

For years the Putnam family followed the Joneses in everything they did. If Jones bought a new car, Putnam felt obligated to buy a new car. If Mrs. Jones bought a new fur coat, Mrs. Putnam had to buy a new fur coat, whether she could afford it or not. When Jones' kid started guitar lessons, Putnam had to give his kid guitar lessons.

It wasn't just Putnam. Everybody on Maple Street felt obliged to keep up with the Joneses.

About a year ago, Putnam came home from his office, tired and irritable, to find a brand-new station wagon in front of Jones' house.

Mrs. Putnam was nervously waiting for her husband. "I called the dealer and ordered a station wagon."

"Why do we have to have a new station wagon?" Putnam demanded.

"What a stupid question to ask," Mrs. Putnam said. "You saw the Joneses' new station wagon outside of their house."

"So what?" said Harry. "Why do we have to do everything they do?"

"Because they are Joneses," his wife said. "You know in America we have to keep up with the Joneses."

"There's no law that says we do," Harry said angrily. "It's just some stupid tradition, and I say the hell with it."

Mrs. Putnam had never seen her husband in such a temper, so she decided to drop the matter.

A few days later Putnam was shoveling the snow off his sidewalk, and Jones, who was using an electric snow-spray machine on his driveway, came over to say hello.

"You ought to get one of these machines, Harry," Jones said. "They're the latest thing."

"I don't need a snow-removal machine," Harry muttered.

Jones ignored Harry's mood and said, "When are you getting delivery on your new station wagon?"

"I'm not buying a new station wagon, Jones."

"But *I* bought one," Jones said.

"Good for you," Harry said. "But we're sticking with last year's car."

"Look, Harry, if it's a question of money," Jones said quietly, "I'll sign a note for you at the bank."

"I don't need you to sign a note for me, Jones," Harry

said. I'm up to here with you. You made me buy a color television set, a garbage crusher, an underwater sprinkling system, a minibike for my son, ballet lessons for my daughter, a trip to Hawaii for my wife, and I had to do over my whole recreation room because you bought a new pool table. I don't care what you do anymore, I'm not going to try and keep up with you."

"Don't yell," pleaded Jones. "The neighbors will hear you."

"I want them to hear me," yelled Harry. "LISTEN, NEIGHBORS, I'M NOT KEEPING UP WITH JONES ANYMORE. HE'S A FOURTEEN-CARAT PHONY, AND HE'S DRIVING US ALL INTO BANKRUPTCY."

The neighbors dashed out on the street. They couldn't believe their ears; no one had ever questioned Jones' status before.

"But if we don't keep up with the Joneses, who are we going to keep up with?" a neighbor asked.

"Me," said Harry. "And for starters, I'm not buying a new station wagon. So I've saved everybody on this block five thousand dollars."

It made sense to the people on Maple Street, and they all voted to keep up with the Putnams instead.

And at that moment the recession in the United States really got under way.

11

FUN AND GAMES

THE PRO FOOTBALL
MURDER MYSTERY

As detective Peter Minderman stared at the color television set in the simple living room of the Socalaw house he was baffled.

The body of Artie Socalaw was still in the same chair where he had died. All the suspects in the case were also in the living room. There was Artie's wife, Emma, and Artie's best friends: George Stevens, Jr., Chuck McDermott, Sam Markay and Tony Valenti.

"All right," said detective Minderman, "let's start from the beginning. You guys began watching pro football two day ago on Saturday at noon, right in this living room."

"That's correct," said Stevens. "Then, suddenly, Sunday night, somewhere during the third quarter of the Raider game, we noticed there was something wrong with Artie. We waited until the game ended at seven and then went over to his chair. He was dead."

"You can imagine what a shock this was, coming after the Forty-Niners' defeat of the Minnesota Vikings," Chuck McDermott added.

"But," said detective Minderman, "the coroner said Artie had been dead for twenty-four hours. How come no one discovered it before then?"

"Well," said Sam Markay, "Artie was always quiet when he watched a pro football game. He wasn't one of these guys who holler and shout after each play. So when he didn't say anything for twenty-four hours, we figured he was just suffering because Dallas beat the Detroit Lions."

"When you're watching pro football on TV," said Tony Valenti, "you don't notice whether people are breathing or not."

Detective Minderman looked over at Mrs. Socalaw. "When did you last see your husband alive?"

"You mean moving around and that sort of thing?" Mrs. Socalaw asked. "I believe it was sometime in July before the exhibition games started. He hasn't left that chair since the Redskins played the Patriots in a preseason game. I don't wish to dispute the coroner's report, but I thought Artie was dead three months ago."

"That's not true," Stevens said. "Just before the Baltimore-Cincinnati game, Artie asked me if I wanted a piece of fruitcake."

"Fruitcake?" detective Minderman said. "Where did the fruitcake come from?"

"I made it," said Mrs. Socalaw. "I always make fruitcake during the holiday season. It helps me forget."

"Did anyone else eat the fruitcake?"

"I did," said McDermott.

"No ill effects?" Minderman asked.

"None that I can tell," McDermott said.

"Damn," said detective Minderman. "There goes the poisoned-fruitcake theory. Did he eat anything else?"

"I gave him a tuna fish sandwich," McDermott said.

"A what?"

"A tuna fish sandwich. You see, Mrs. Socalaw refuses to feed us, so we each bring our own food. This time my wife made me a tuna fish sandwich."

"But don't you know what's going on with tuna fish?" Minderman asked.

"I'm not much for fishing. The only sport I watch is football," McDermott said.

"Your wife tried to knock you off with a tuna fish mercury-poisoned sandwich," detective Minderman said. "Only Artie became the victim, instead of you."

"I knew she was sore at me," McDermott said, "but I didn't think she'd go this far."

Minderman went to the phone and called the McDermott house. "Mrs. McDermott, I'm sending someone over to arrest you for the tuna fish murder of Artie Socalaw."

"Don't worry, Gloria," Mrs. Socalaw, grabbing the phone, shouted, "I'll testify in your behalf. We can always say it was a crime of passion."

SUMMER READING

With the summer coming up, we recommend the following books for light reading:

Everything You Wanted To Know About Socks (But Were Afraid to Ask). Dr. David Suphose has written the first frank, uncensored book about socks, which tells you not only how to get more pleasure out of your socks but how to wear them without hang-ups or guilt. This book answers the question as to when to wear socks and with whom. There are chapters titled "Is Darning Unhealthy?" "Exciting Things to Do with Your Ankles," "Erogenous Parts of Your Heel," and "Pre-Sock Foreplay," which deals with the pleasure you can get from your toes before putting on your socks.

For the first time, a distinguished American writer has put forth the proposition that everyone is entitled to a really joyous and fulfilling sock life, and if your feet can find happiness, the rest of you won't be far behind.

Up Against the Kindergarten Wall. Haspel Short, age six, kept a diary of last spring's famous takeover of the Hawthorne kindergarten. This is the first version told from the student's point of view. The kindergarten riots started over a small thing. The administration switched from chocolate milk to white milk at the eleven o'clock cookie hour, without informing the pupils. Several of the students refused to drink the white milk, so their teacher, Miss Jean Brodie, reported them to the principal, Marcus Chips. When Chips came to the class and warned that anyone who did not drink white milk would be expelled, one of the students shouted, "Good-bye, Marcus."

Chips had no choice but to call out the National Guard, which radicalized everyone, even the students who preferred white milk over chocolate milk.

Short writes with both humor and despair and makes the point that perhaps because we have taken our milk program in kindergarten for granted for so long, we are reaping the whirlwind at last.

The Godmother, by Mario Whuzo, is a very exciting novel about the head of the ladies' auxiliary of Mafia Lodge No. 8. Rosina Nirvana started as a young girl repairing bulletproof vests for a large family in Brooklyn.

She becomes the protégée of Nostra Maria, who rolled bandages for the Luchese brothers. One day Nostra Maria is found in the East River with a sewing machine tied around her neck, and Rosina Nirvana becomes the godmother of the ladies' auxiliary.

The novel tells with sympathy and understanding what it's like for the women who sit and wait while their husbands are away collecting bad debts.

Sworn to suffer in silence, the women devote themselves to good deeds, holding benefits for the widows and orphans of the stool pigeons their men were forced to send to that big Godmother in the Sky.

President for a Week. George Shrimpton, who has played football with the New York Giants, fought Cassius Clay, conducted the Bolshoi Theater, and hijacked a plane to Cuba, has written his funniest book to date about being President of the United States. Shrimpton persuaded President Nixon to stay down at Key Biscayne for a week while he ran the country. Naturally everything Shrimpton did was wrong.

One hilarious incident follows another. First he locks Billy Graham out of the White House. Then he accidentally hooks up the CIA telephone with the hot line to Moscow, and then he takes over the controls of Air Force I and almost gets shot down over Peking.

His final ignominious hour comes when he declares the Fourth of July a working day for government employees and spoils President Nixon's only chance to bring the country together. (Nonfiction.)

FOR THE ENTIRE FAMILY

One of the problems of taking children on vacation is that there is nothing to do with them in the evenings. There is one movie house in our town on Cape Cod, and it shows a different film every night. Unfortunately none of the children has been able to go because every film that they've shown has been graded by the Valenti code as M for mature audiences only, R for restricted audiences only, or X which means you have to prove you're dirty old men before they let you in.

You can therefore imagine my surprise when I heard the other day the Bijou Cinema was advertising for Saturday night a G picture, which meant it was for the entire family. I couldn't believe it, so I ran down to the theater to see if it was possibly true.

Other parents had also heard the rumor, and there was a large crowd in front of the building staring at the coming-attractions poster which said the film on Saturday had been declared for general audiences "without any restrictions."

"What could it possibly be?" a father next to me said.

"I don't know," I admitted. "I thought they had given up making films for the entire family."

"Maybe it's a foreign film," his wife suggested.

"It could be an old M-G-M film that they retitled," another man said. "I'm sure Hollywood wouldn't make a new film for children to see."

A lady became indignant. "They should have given us some advance notice. I had a big dinner planned for Saturday evening and now I have to cancel it."

"Why?" a man asked.

"I've never seen a movie for general audiences, and another one may not come along for years," she said.

Apparently word had spread beyond the town because people were driving in from the countryside to see the poster. Main Street was clogged with cars, and fathers were standing in the middle of the street holding their children on their shoulders so they could get a better look at the G rating.

The manager of the movie house came out perspiring. "Please go home. This is Thursday, and the family movie isn't scheduled until Saturday night. You're hurting my regular business."

Nobody moved. "How do we know we can get in on Saturday night?" a man shouted.

"Yeah," someone else yelled, "suppose the whole Cape hears you're showing a G movie? We won't be able to get in. Why can't we buy our tickets now?"

The crowd was becoming ugly. The manager got up on a box. "Please," he said, "it's not my fault. We're only permitted to show one film for the entire family each summer. If it was up to me, I'd show another one, though heaven knows where I'd find it."

A mother cried, "We support you when you show your M and R movies. Why can't we get some consideration when you show a G movie?"

"How about a matinee?" I suggested. "In that way more people could see it."

"I can't show it at a matinee. Next Saturday's matinee is already booked for *I Am Curious (Yellow)*."

"My child's never seen a movie," another mother cried. "Couldn't children who have never seen a movie be given first preference?"

"Madam," the manager said. "We can't cater to lower age groups."

It looked hopeless, so I decided to go home. As I suspected, the word had spread all along the Cape that our cinema was going to show a family movie, and on Friday morning caravans of people started to arrive with tents and sleeping bags.

By Saturday morning people had abandoned their cars 20 miles from the town and walked on foot in hopes of seeing it. By Saturday afternoon the place looked like the Woodstock Festival at Bethel, New York. The Bijou Cinema has only 500 seats, so 60,000 people had to be turned away from the theater. But they didn't seem to mind.

The father of one tribe said as he tied up his bedroll, "I think just being in town where they were showing a film for the entire family, even if we didn't get in, was a wonderful experience for the kids."

ADULT MOVIES

It is obvious the motion picture companies in Hollywood are in trouble. The major studios are trying to outdo each other, making films about revolution, dope and sex in a desperate effort to attract the two major groups who still go to the movies—young people and dirty old men.

Sampson P. Truberry, head of MTA (Miserable Twentieth Arts) studios, told me, "The motion picture industry has come of age. We are now making adult pictures which tell it like it is. The days of *Sound of Music* and *Gone with the Wind* are over."

Truberry continued, "When I took over this studio a year ago, we were losing ten million dollars a month. I made three movies—*Motorcycle Virgin, Key Club* and *Molotov Cocktail*—and now we're in the black. The studio is booming now. Come on, I'll take you around."

We went to Stage 5. As we came on the set, there were a man and woman taking a bath. Truberry whispered to me, "This is one of our big Christmas pictures. It's Christmas Eve, and they've just finished trimming the tree, so they've decided to take a bath together."

"Are they married?" I whispered back.

Truberry shook his head. "They're brother and sister, dummy."

"I should have known."

Truberry said, "You see the director? He's the hottest thing in Hollywood. He used to make stag movies for fraternity houses, was arrested seven times, did six years in prison. Now he gets half a million dollars a picture, and we've got him signed for five."

Someone yelled, "Quiet on the set!" and we walked over to Stage 9. When we opened the door, a din of rock music almost knocked us off our feet.

This time Truberry had to shout, "This one's titled *Beyond the Valley of Woodstock*. Everyone's stoned in the movie from the beginning to end."

"What's the story?" I shouted back.

"There's no story, dumb-dumb," he shouted. "Everyone does his own thing."

The smoke from the pot was getting to me, so I went outside to get some fresh air. Truberry followed. "They never knew how to make pictures like this in the old days," he said.

While we were standing there, we heard fire engines and saw a gigantic blaze pouring out of the administration building of the studio. We ran toward it and saw a wild young man screaming into a megaphone: "Keep those fire trucks out of the way. We're shooting a scene!"

Truberry ran up to him. "Jerry, what the hell are you doing?"

"We're shooting the final scene of *Down with Everything*. It's a helluva blaze, huh, boss?"

"There was nothing in the script about you burning down the administration building."

"We're improvising. Man, what a finish!"

An assistant director ran up. "Jerry, do you want to throw some dummy bodies on the fire?"

"Are you kidding? There is nothing fake about this movie. Throw in Truberry here."

Two grips picked up Truberry and started carrying him toward the fire as he screamed.

"Let's get it right on the first take!" Jerry yelled into his megaphone. "We may not find anyone to do it again."

WHAT NOT TO SAY

The Women's Liberation people take themselves very seriously, and well they might. It's very hard to say anything to them without getting them very mad. While I have no idea what you *should* say to someone in Women's Lib, here are some of the things you should *not* say:

"Well, now that you've got your college degree, I suppose you're going to find yourself a husband."

"You ought to meet Hugh Hefner—he's your kind of guy."

"How do you like this picture of the sexy girl in a bathing suit?"

"Have you heard the latest one about the woman driver who—"

"What's the name of your hairdresser?"

"I suppose if you take this job, you'll probably become pregnant."

"You women go in the other room. We'll stay here for cigars and cognac."

"Wouldn't you hate to be married to a man who makes as much money as you do?"

"Here, let me light your cigarette for you."

"For a woman, you play very well."

"My mother always did something stupid like that herself."

"There's a gal in our office who is as good at selling as any man."

"Hey, look, there's a lady taxi driver!"

"We'd be happy to let you in the press box—it's just that we don't have any lavatory facilities."

"Ha-ha-ha . . . A woman President, that's a good one. Ho-ho-ho."

"Would you like to go out to Ladies' Day at the ball park?"

"The thing I like about you the best is your legs."

"I met this woman doctor the other day, at the hospital, and she really seemed to know what she was doing."

"What do you think about when you're having a baby?"

"I beg your pardon, ma'am. Is the head of the house home?"

"Would you like to feel my muscle?"

"Show me a woman who really likes working, and I'll show you a woman who likes other women."

"A penny for your thoughts."

"Hi, how's the better half feeling?"

"Don't feel bad, I even know men who don't understand it."

"No, sit down and join us. We have nothing important to say."

"The newspaper just arrived. Would you like the women's page?"

"Listen, I'm the first one to admit women have gotten a raw deal, but the majority of them wouldn't have it any other way."

"Meet me at the ladies' entrance of the club at five o'clock."

Any of the above statements can cause a Women's Lib backer to get uptight, but if you really want to see her climb the wall start singing:

> "You've come a long way, baby,
> "To get where you got to today.
> "You've got your own cigarette now, baby,
> "You've come a long, long way."

TAHITIAN WOMEN'S LIB

Women's liberation is working in Tahiti as well as, or better than, any place in the world. I discovered this when I visited the beautiful island of Bora-Bora, which inspired James Michener's *Tales of the South Pacific*. We stayed at the Hotel Bora-Bora, where, instead of hotel rooms, each couple has its own grass-covered hut overlooking the crystal-clear fish-happy lagoon.

One of the first things I noticed was that there were

only women working in the hotel, at the desk or the bar, as chambermaids or waitresses.

One morning I made a discreet inquiry as to where all the men on Bora-Bora were.

A Frenchman who lives on the island said, "They're probably still in their huts sleeping. They're very tired celebrating the Fourteenth of July which, as you know, has been going on for ten days."

"But don't they have to go to work?"

"No, monsieur. The tradition of the islands is that only the women work."

"What do the men do?"

"Sleep, sail, fish if they feel like it. They manage to keep busy."

"But if the women work, what do the men use for money?"

"The women give them the money they make."

"But that's wonderful," I said. "This is a country of true women's liberation."

"It has its advantages," the Frenchman said.

"Who takes care of the children?"

"The women."

"Who does the cooking, cleaning and washing?"

"The women. You see, monsieur, the men here respect their women and let them do *everything*. As a matter of fact, there aren't enough hours in the day for a woman to fulfill herself."

"What about marriage?"

"Some people get married, some don't. If a man tires of his woman, he can find another one."

"Then a woman here does not have to be tied down."

"No. As soon as her man leaves her, she is free."

"This is a women's lib paradise," I said. "It must make the men angry to know the women have all the jobs."

"Not really. You must understand that the Tahitian man is not as ambitious as the American. Many, many years ago, Tahitian men discovered that there wasn't anything they could do that their women couldn't do better.

Once they made this discovery, they decided it was stupid to compete with them."

"If only American men could learn this," I said, "we would indeed have a happy country."

"I do not want to give the impression the men do not work at all. Many of them play musical instruments when their wives dance for the tourists."

"You mean after they work all day, cook, clean, and take care of their children, the women still have time to dance for the tourists?"

"Of course," the Frenchman said. "It is part of their duties. The tourists would be very disappointed to come all this way and not see the Tahitian women dance."

"To think," I said, "they've managed to have all this liberation without a revolution."

"It is a unique position for women to hold, but even in paradise there is trouble. A few women are complaining that they are *too* liberated. They're starting to demand less rights and more time off."

VIOLENCE IS TAXABLE

My friend McCormick thinks he has an answer to all the violence in movies and on television.

"Tax the hell out of them," he said.

"But how?" I asked.

"You sell licenses to producers of movies and television shows. They'd be like a hunting permit. You wouldn't be allowed to kill anyone in a TV program or a film without first buying a license. It would cost you one thousand dollars to kill one man, two thousand to kill a woman, and five thousand if you wanted to kill a child."

"Would you have a limit on how many people you could bag?"

"Not at the beginning. I think a producer could kill as many people as he wanted to, providing he had a license for each one."

"What about the method of killing people in movies and TV?"

"We might add a surcharge for unorthodox methods of killing, such as burning, garroting, and throwing them off buildings. But I believe shooting or stabbing should be permitted for the straight thousand-dollar fee."

"McCormick, your idea has great merit, but it seems to me it would add tremendous costs to cowboy pictures."

"Exactly. I believe the producers of cowboy films and TV shows would have to be very discriminating in whom they killed. It will stop them from shooting everyone within camera range. If, for example, a producer had only three licenses, he'd have to choose his victims pretty carefully."

"It would certainly save a lot of Indians from being killed," I said.

"As far as war pictures are concerned, we might make a package deal. For a flat one hundred thousand dollars the producers would be permitted to wipe out either one World War Two German battalion or sink one Japanese aircraft carrier with all personnel on board."

"Would you require licenses for wounding and maiming people on TV and in films?"

"I would propose a rate card starting with knocking out a person in a fist fight, which would cost ten dollars, to causing a severe brain concussion, which would cost the producer five hundred. Any open wound or display of blood would automatically be taxed an extra one hundred."

"It seems to me those prices are pretty high."

"That's the idea. The only way you're going to get anyone to cut down on violence is to hit him where it hurts—in the pocketbook."

"At the same time," McCormick continued, "I believe producers of nonviolent films should be encouraged by receiving tax rebates. If anyone makes a TV show or picture in which no one is either killed or maimed, he certainly deserves all the tax advantages he can get."

"You've really thought this through," I said.

"It's going to be a tough fight to get it by Congress," McCormick said.

208

"How's that?"

"The pro-violence lobby in Washington has put out the word that if anyone taxes violence, he'll soon be wearing cement shoes."

12

WHERE NIXON WENT WRONG

THE SOLUTION TO WELFARE

One of the major political issues in the 1972 political campaign is going to be welfare. The American worker is furious at those who collect money for doing nothing. Governor Ronald Reagan was the first to sense welfare as the nation's number one "gut" issue, and now President Nixon has decided to run with it.

In a speech to Republican governors, the President discussed the welfare picture and mentioned that one of the things wrong with welfare is that people would rather take money from the government than work at what they considered "menial" jobs.

The President told his audience, "Scrubbing floors or emptying bedpans—my mother used to do that—is not enjoyable work, but a lot of people do it, and there is as much dignity in that as there is in any other work to be done in this country—including my own."

My friend Sid Liebes, who works out at Stanford as a physicist, has been giving a lot of thought to the problem of menial work and how we can get people who are on welfare to take it.

He said, "What President Nixon says about menial jobs having as much dignity as his work is just not so. Have you ever seen a band play 'Hail to the Chief' when someone empties a bedpan?"

"Not since I've been in Washington," I admitted.

"To solve the problem of getting people willing to go off welfare to take menial work such as cleaning, scrubbing and washing dirty dishes, you have to understand something about the nature of work. It is a scientific fact that the higher people are in an organization, the happier they are in what they're doing.

"The secretary is happier than the cleaning woman, the sales manager is happier than the secretary, the vice-president is happier than the sales manager, and the president and chairman of the board are presumably happier at their work than anybody else."

Liebes continued, "There are exceptions, but as a rule this holds true. Most successful people say they wouldn't want to do anything else. The lower down on the ladder, the more complaining you hear, until you get to the stockroom, where the turnover is frightening.

"The one thing we all know is that people have to feel they're doing something important or they just won't work."

"What do you propose?"

"The Liebes Plan," he said. "I suggest that we reverse the salary scales so that the people who are doing the most menial work get the highest pay.

"For example, the cleaning woman would start at seventy-five thousand dollars a year; her immediate superior, the floor waxer, would get sixty thousand dollars a year; a secretary would get fifty thousand dollars a year; and so on, all the way up the line until you reached the president of the company, who would get thirty-five hundred a year. The worst jobs in this country would pay the most.

"Since the people on top are happy in what they're doing, they don't need large sums of money to persuade them they're contributing to society."

"But wait a minute, Liebes," I said. "If the people on top only make thirty-five hundred dollars a year, they might quit and go on welfare."

"Never," Liebes said. "Only the people in the upper classes still consider it a disgrace to go eat at the government trough."

"There should be a hole in your plan," I said. "But I can't see one."

"It's foolproof," he replied. "Once you make menial jobs the highest-paying ones, you solve your welfare problem overnight. Show me a street cleaner making fifty thousands dollars a year and I'll show you someone with as much dignity as the President of the United States."

INCOME TAX DAY

Income Tax Day is probably the most important joyous holiday in the United States and observed by everyone, regardless of race, creed, religion, or color. While everyone pays tribute to it, few people know how Income Tax Day came about.

The father of the income tax was born on April 15, 1842, to Mr. and Mrs. Hiram Tax of Washington, D.C. His parents named him Maxwel Tax, but to his family and friends he became known as Max Tax.

Max was a bright boy and studied very hard at school. He wanted to become a doctor, but his parents thought he should be an accountant. In those days you did what your parents told you to do, and so Max, at twenty-one, became a certified public accountant.

But Max soon discovered there wasn't enough for accountants to do, and he couldn't find any people in Washington who would let him keep their books.

Every time he approached a company or an individual, he was asked, "Who needs you?"

Max became embittered, and he decided that someday people would rue their words. He set out to devise a plan that would make every person in the United States dependent on accountants from the day they were born until the day they died.

But how?

One day in 1862 he attended a speech given by President Abraham Lincoln on the White House lawn.

Mr. Lincoln said sadly, in one part of his speech, "You can tax some of the people all the time, and all of the people some of the time. But you can't tax all of the people all the time."

These words stuck with Max, and that night he kept mulling it over in his mind. At three o'clock in the morning, he sat up in his bed and shouted, "Eureka!"

His wife, Tina, said, "Max what is it?"

"Tina, I think I've got it. I believe I have a way of

making us rich for the rest of our lives. Lincoln needs money desperately. If we could put a levy on everyone's salary in this country, the government would have more money than it would know what to do with."

"But how would that help us, Max?" Tina asked.

"The government would make this levy so complicated that only accountants would be able to figure it out. If people didn't hire us, they would go to jail."

Max went down to his basement for two weeks and worked on a form that only accountants could understand.

Then he went to see President Lincoln. At first Lincoln was appalled by the idea.

"The oil lobby would never let it through," Lincoln said.

"We'll exempt oil people," Max said.

"All right," Lincoln said, "I'll buy it. And because you came up with the idea, I'll call it the Max Income Tax Plan." (The Max was later dropped because there was no room on the form.)

As Max predicted, the demand for accountants was so great after the law was passed that he became a millionaire overnight. He also was asked to lecture all over the world on his plan. England was so grateful to him that they knighted him, and he has been known in that country as Sir Tax.

But unfortunately, Max was so busy lecturing, entertaining, and working on other people's income taxes that he forgot to file his own. One day the IRS confiscated everything he owned, and in a few years he was a broken, penniless, bitter man. Because his plan caused so many people so much anguish, he died without a friend in the world.

It was only after his death that a grateful government decided to pay homage to him. By Presidential decree, April 15 was declared Income Tax Day, and each year on that day the Secretary of the Treasury places a wreath on Max's unmarked grave.

Max Tax is long since gone, but his name is on the lips of all of us.

CHILDREN OF YOUR CHOICE

Science is now fiddling with animal sperm banks. It is already possible through deepfreeze methods to save the reproductive ingredients of a great bull for several years and then, by artificial insemination, to produce a calf whose father may have long gone on to that great cow pasture in the sky.

Lucy Kavaler in the New York *Times* has suggested that if there are now banks for animals, we should start thinking in terms of human beings. She suggests that the reproductive cells of great men could be frozen and banked for future generations.

Miss Kavaler foresees a time, in the not too distant future, when a man and wife would be able to do down to their local test tube bank and select the child of their dreams.

So do we.

It is the year 2001, and a couple walks into the First National Test Tube Bank of New York. They are ushered into an icebox, where the vice-president, bundled up in a sheepskin coat, asks them to state their business.

The wife says, "I would like either another Artur Rubinstein or a Jascha Heifetz."

"But," says the husband, "he should be able to throw a football like Joe Namath."

The vice-president says, "We're all out of Artur Rubinsteins, Jascha Heifetzes, and Joe Namaths. The last of them went in 1996. Could I interest you in a Norman Mailer or an Erich Segal?"

The husband says, "If you don't have a Joe Namath, what about a good linebacker?"

The wife says, "I want my son to be a professional man. Maybe a doctor. You don't have a Jonas Salk sample around, do you?"

"No, I'm sorry," the vice-president replies. "The last genes of Jonas Salk went in 1987."

"I tell you what," says the husband, "if you have a good golfer like Arnold Palmer, we'll take it."

"Not so fast," the wife says. "Golfers are a dime a dozen. I would like perhaps a little artistic genius. Maybe a Pablo Picasso or a Chagall."

"Wait a minute," the husband says. "The Martons got a Picasso twenty years ago, but instead of him painting pictures, he became a Communist and got married three times."

"Well," says the vice-president, "there is no guarantee that your offspring will not inherit *all* the characteristics of the person you choose."

"Don't I know it!" the wife says. "The Kaisers had a Dr. Edward Teller offspring, and he married a daughter who came from a General Patton strain, and now all they want to do is make war instead of love."

The vice-president studies a list. "Would you consider a politician for a son? We're having a sale on John Lindsay."

"Not on your life," the husband says. "Anyone who wants his son to be mayor of New York has to be crazy."

"I wouldn't be adverse to an Onassis-type child," the wife says. "At least we wouldn't have to worry about security in our old age."

The vice-president says, "We've been sold out of Onassis for twenty years. Why do you think there's such a glut in oil tankers these days?"

The husband says, "Maybe we should try for a basketball player."

The wife says angrily, "I'm not going to produce a seven-foot giant just so you can go to Madison Square Garden three nights a week."

The vice-president says, "You people are going to have to make up your minds."

The wife says, "All right, give us a Ralph Nader. He may not get rich, but at least he'll always tell us the truth."

BROTHER, CAN YOU SPARE $100?

The Washington social season has never been more fraught with cocktail parties, dinner parties, autograph parties and testimonials, all in the name of political fund raising. People in this town live in fear every time the mail arrives that among the bills and junk letters will be buried an invitation to someone's house for a friendly drink.

This drink can cost the invitee anywhere from $25 to $500 as a political contribution to some poor Senator or Congressman's campaign.

Last week was typical of what is going on here. On Monday I arrived home and my wife said, "The Jessels have invited us for cocktails tomorrow night to meet Senator Bolt."

"Who wants to meet him?" I said. "I saw him last night at a fund-raising party for Congressman Ax."

"Well, we can't say no. I run into Ginny Jessel at the hairdresser's every week, and she'll think we couldn't afford fifty dollars to come to her party."

The next night, as we were getting dressed for the Jessel bash, my wife said, "There's an autograph party for Senator Finney at the Quagmires tomorrow."

"An autograph party?"

"Yes. Senator Finney is autographing his new book, *The Sensuous Senator*. If you contribute one hundred dollars, he'll sign it to you personally."

"One hundred dollars? I wouldn't buy it if it was printed in paperback."

"Well, the Quagmires reminded me that they gave us one hundred dollars for the Junior Village Telethon, and so I said we'd come."

A few nights later I was home reading my autographed copy of *The Sensuous Senator* when a telegram arrived. It read, "YOU ARE INVITED TO A TESTIMONIAL DINNER CELEBRATING CONGRESSMAN ALF KLOTZNICK'S 30TH ANNIVERSARY AS A MEM-

218

BER OF THE HOUSE DISTRICT SEWER COMMIT-
TEE. A TABLE HAS BEEN RESERVED IN YOUR
NAME. PLEASE MAKE OUT A $150 CHECK IN
NAME OF KLOTZNICK-FOR-CONGRESS COMMIT-
TEE."

"Now they've gone too far," I said to my wife. "I
wouldn't be caught dead at a testimonial for Klotznick."

"You can say that now," my wife said. "But the next
time our sewer breaks, Klotznick will block the bill to
fix it in his committee."

We had no choice but to go to Klotznick's testimonial.

For two days after that we didn't get any invitations to
go out, and I was starting to worry that we had been
crossed off everybody's list.

But on the third evening, when I came home from the
office, my wife said, "Guess what?"

"I'm not going to any more cocktail parties, autograph
parties or testimonial dinners this year, and that is final,"
I yelled.

"You don't have to go to any," she said nervously.

"Great."

"Sally Fowler called and asked if we could come to a
brunch on Sunday for Forest, who is running against
Senator Boots Kimberly. I told her how you hated to go
out on Sundays, so she asked if we could hold it here."

"You wouldn't," I said.

"Well, now that we owe the Jessels and the Quagmires,
it will be an easy way to get even."

IT'S WHO LOSES THAT COUNTS

Have you ever wondered what happens to a person who
loses an election in the United States? It isn't a pretty
sight to see.

"Hello, is this the AFL-CIO headquarters? I'd like to
speak to Mr. Novak . . . Mr. Novak, this is Jerry Collenberg . . . C-O-L-L-E-N-B-E-R-G. That's right . . . You
remember I was running for Congressman from the Second Congressional District? . . . Well, as you know, I

lost and . . . J-E-R-R-Y Collenberg . . . We had lunch together and you told me how pleased you were that someone with new blood was in the race . . . We did, too, have lunch together! Hal Walker, my campaign manager, was with me . . . You don't remember it? You said labor was very interested in defeating my opponent and you would do anything to help . . . Well, Mr. Novak, I'm sorry I didn't win, but what I was calling about was that I have this fifty-thousand-dollar deficit and I was wondering if . . . Mr. Novak! Mr. Novak! . . . Operator, we've been cut off."

"Hello, is this the National Association of Machine-Gun Manufacturers? Do you have a lobbyist named Thompson? Could you please connect me . . . Mr. Thompson, this is Jerry Collenberg . . . C-O-L-L-E-N-B-E-R-G . . . Oh, you remember me? . . . Yes, thank you very much. I was hoping to do better, but my opponent out-spent me two to one . . . I have a letter in front of me from you indicating that the National Association of Machine-Gun Manufacturers was interested in my race and I replied that I was very flattered that you even knew I was running . . . You got my letter? . . . Good . . . Mr. Thompson, I have a deficit of fifty thousand dollars, and I was wondering if the NAMGM would be willing to help out . . . What's that? . . . You never contribute to Congressional elections?

"I know it's against the law, Mr. Thompson, but you indicated in your letter that individuals in the machine-gun business were willing to make personal contributions to my campaign . . . It's right here in your letter . . . Mr. Thompson, I'm not asking you to do anything dishonest . . . Mr. Thompson, I'd like to read one phrase from your letter . . . you said, and I quote, 'As far as the machine-gun manufacturers in this country are concerned, the sky's the limit when it comes to getting you elected.' . . . I'm not asking for the sky . . . I'm asking for a small financial contribution to wipe out my deficit . . . no, I don't need a machine gun. . . ."

"Dr. Bartlett, this is Jerry Collenberg . . . You discussed with me the dangers of socialized medicine last month

. . . Yes, I appreciate that, Doctor, but my opponent made some ruthless charges and I never had the money to answer . . . Doctor, you told me that the medical association had a political fund for candidates who were sympathetic to the medical profession . . . You do recall our conversation? Then, do you remember saying you were going to send me a check for two thousand dollars to further my campaign? . . . You don't remember that? . . . I was afraid you wouldn't . . . Good-bye."

"Hello, Harry . . . I understand perfectly well why you didn't call after the election . . . I'm not sore, honest . . . Of course you were busy . . . Harry, when I got into this race, you came to me and said it was the greatest moment in your life, and that you'd stand by me whether I won or lost . . . I was wondering if there was any chance of getting together a committee to help me with my deficit? . . . Oh, you're going skiing? . . . Well, when you come back from skiing? . . .

"You don't know when you're getting back? I see . . . It's okay, Harry, of course I know you'd help if you could . . . You'd like to send me a check for twenty-five dollars . . . Are you sure you can spare it? . . . I'm not being sarcastic . . . What are you getting mad at me for? I'm the one who lost the election. . . ."

"Hello? Yes, dear . . . What's happening? They've come for the furniture . . . who's come for the furniture? . . . The advertising agency that ran my campaign . . . Oh, God, stall them. I'll call party headquarters . . . Surely they'll help us out."

"Hello, let me speak to the party treasurer . . . It's an emergency . . . Jerry Collenberg . . . J-E-R-R-Y C-O-L-L-E-N-B-E-R-G."

THE DON'T KNOWS ARE RIDING HIGH

In election years, the only people who seem to know their own minds are those who keep telling the pollsters they don't know for whom they are going to vote.

"The 'don't-know' vote," said Heinrich Applebaum, the

leading elections expert in the United States, "could easily swing this country one way or the other."

"Do you mean to say the 'don't-know' vote is bigger than the Middle America vote?"

"It's even bigger than the silent majority," Applebaum replied. "We estimate that for every person in this country who knows whom he is going to vote for, there are two and one-half persons who don't know."

"How do you explain such a large 'don't-know' vote?"

"The 'don't-know' voters are made up of people who are sick and tired of being told whom they should vote for. They're the true Americans who are being pushed around by everybody. They pay their taxes, send their kids to school, watch television, drink beer, salute the flag, and yet when it comes to elections, they have no idea what the hell the candidate is talking about."

"Wasn't there always a large 'don't-know' segment in the population?" I asked.

"Nothing comparable to what we have at the present time. In the past no one wanted to admit he didn't know what was going on in the country. Now if you refuse to admit you don't know, people think you should be taken away to the funny farm."

Applebaum said the "don't knows" could be ethnically broken down among those who are "undecided," "unsure," and have "no opinion."

"These three groups compose the majority of the 'don't-know' voters," he said.

"What's the difference between them?"

"The 'undecided' are those in the five-thousand-to-fifteen-thousand-dollar-a-year income bracket. They are mostly white, though a few are Inca Indians."

"I see."

"The 'unsure' are mostly composed of hard hats, blue-collar workers and Avon ladies. While they're working, this group seem to know exactly whom they are for. It's when they get laid off because of a recession that they get confused."

"And the 'no opinion'?"

"The people who express 'no opinion' are those who

don't want to be identified with those who are 'undecided' or 'unsure.' "

"I see."

"In the past, the 'undecideds' and the 'unsures' and those with 'no opinion' always split their votes. But this year, because of the low quality of the campaigns and lack of issues, all three groups might vote together, and this could have a tremendous effect on the nation."

"Why doesn't Agnew appeal to the 'don't knows'?"

"Because his whole campaign has been aimed at the 'know nothings.' It's easy for someone like Agnew to get the two mixed up."

"Why don't the 'don't knows' put up their own candidate if they're that strong?"

"If they proposed their own candidate, they could no longer be identified with those who were 'undecided,' 'unsure' and had 'no opinion.' The best the 'don't knows' can hope for is that the election will be called off in November because of inclement weather."

LET'S PAUSE FOR A MOMENT

I don't know if people have noticed it, but TV political commercials are getting nastier and nastier. There was a time when a candidate appeared on the screen and made a one-minute pitch for your vote. But all this has gone by the boards, and now, thanks to the great creative brains of our advertising media, the new approach is to tell the audience what a miserable s.o.b. the candidate's opponent is.

I sat in on a session where the top advertising men were brainstorming a TV commercial campaign for their candidate, Philbus Wurm, who was running for the U.S. Senate against the incumbent, Senator Allegro Symphony.

This is how it went:

"As I see it," said the copywriter, "we have to sell the people on Symphony's softness on pornography. Now, what I suggest we do is have a woman sleeping in bed, and a guy comes in and rapes her, and the voice-over says,

'These are the people Senator Symphony wants to let into your bedroom.' "

"Not enough shock value," the art director said. "How about this? A group of dirty, hairy students sneak up to a building and plant a bomb. The bomb goes off, and the voice-over says, 'Symphony voted for the last education bill.' "

"That's not bad," said a vice-president. "I thought we might use a lot of footage from the California brush fires. You know, homes burning and stuff like that, and then a shot of Symphony playing a violin, which he does. The voice-over could say, 'Nero wasn't the only one who fiddled.' "

"That's great," another vp said. "How about Vietnam?"

"We've been working on that," the copywriter said. "We have some stock footage of a GI platoon attacking Hill 2,331. Then we hear Symphony's voice saying, 'Vietnam was a big mistake,' and the voice-over says, 'Tell it to Company D.' "

The campaign manager was ecstatic. "Beautiful. You have anything on the economy?"

The art director says, "We have some footage of an unemployment office, and we go in close on a guy who is holding his check, and we say, 'Why are you out of a job?' and he says, 'Because Senator Symphony closed the naval base.' Then we show a crew putting the guy's furniture out in the street."

"Did you tell him about the hunger ad?" a vice-president asked.

"Not yet," the copywriter said. "We show this family at a table and the mother says to her children, 'All we have to eat tonight is turnips.' Then we fade and show Symphony eating spaghetti at an Italian saint's day festival and the voice-over says, 'Mamma mia! That's a meatball.' "

The art director said, "I think you'll like this one. It portrays Washington going up in a mushroom cloud and then a bunch of Soviet officers laughing. The voice-over says, 'Senator Symphony voted against the ABM.' "

224

"It's dirty, but it will sell," the campaign manager said, laughing.

"But what about our candidate, Philbus Wurm?" someone asked. "Don't you think we ought to make *one* commercial with him in it?"

"Hell, no. If anyone sees that idiot on TV, we'll lose all our votes."

WHERE NIXON WENT WRONG

The question that everyone is trying to figure out is where the Nixon strategy went wrong. Heinrich Applebaum, elite professor of political science at Moribund University, believes he can pinpoint the exact moment when President Nixon lost his chance to gain control of the U.S. Senate and House of Representatives.

Applebaum told me, "My surveys indicated that up until the Sunday morning before election day, President Nixon had it made. The violence issue, thanks to San Jose, had taken hold, and an indignant nation was waiting to go to the polls and vote out those candidates whom both Nixon and Agnew indicated were permissivists who condoned student unrest. I have never seen a better orchestrated campaign, and I was willing to cede the Senate and House to the Republicans."

"But what happened, Professor, to change the picture?"

"The pro football games. That's what happened."

"I don't understand."

"The Republicans bought time on both NBC and CBS for a special political appeal by President Nixon to be aired between half times of all the pro football games in the country. It was a blunder of colossal proportions."

"I don't understand."

"Who watches football on Sunday in the United States?"

"The silent majority," I said.

"Exactly. The very backbone of this country. Now the silent majority is willing to listen to anything the President of the United States has to say six days a week. But Sunday they set aside to watch football. They don't want

225

to hear about the Vietnamese war, the economy, law and order or violence in the streets. All they want to do is drink their cans of beer and watch two football teams try to kill each other on the gridiron."

"That isn't asking much," I said.

"Up until half time, the silent majority was willing to vote the straight Nixon-Agnew slate," Applebaum said.

"But, suddenly, President Nixon appeared on millions of screens all over the country. The silent majority couldn't believe it. They were expecting to see a half-time show with a marching band, drum majorettes, baton twirlers and all the things that make pro football worth watching.

"In fury, they changed to the other channel, only to discover President Nixon had also bought time between the half of *that* game. And, instead of talking about football, Nixon was discussing politics."

"It takes a lot to get the silent majority angry," Applebaum said. "But this was too much. When you mess around with their football games on Sunday, you're hitting them where it hurts.

"All over the country people started throwing beer cans at their television sets. Husbands began screaming at their wives. Kids began to cry. By the time the President finished making his appeal, he lost all the goodwill he had picked up in his three weeks of arduous campaigning. The silent majority decided anyone who was that insensitive to pro-football watching on Sunday afternoon could just go whistle 'Dixie.' "

"But, wait a minute, Professor. The Democrats also bought spots at half time, and actor E. G. Marshall and Democratic Chairman Lawrence O'Brien made a pitch for their party."

"No one knew who they were," Applebaum said. "The silent majority thought they were doing a meatball commercial for Alka-Seltzer."

WOMEN'S LIB ON
MARTHA'S VINEYARD

Each person celebrated Women's Liberation Day in her own way, and even on a beautiful island such as Martha's Vineyard the women protested in their fashion.

I hadn't even realized it was Women's Liberation Day until I got to the tennis court and my wife said at the start of a doubles game, "I'm not going to serve today."

"What do you mean you're not going to serve? You have to serve."

"I'm sick and tired of serving all the time," she said.

"But if you don't serve, we can't play."

"Aha," she said. "That's the first time you've even acknowledged that my serving meant something."

"I've always admired your serve," I said. "You serve very well."

"Well, I'm not serving today. You can serve for the both of us."

I looked hopelessly across the net at the Styrons, who were in a serious argument.

"You ready?" I asked.

"Rose says she's not going to serve today," Styron yelled. Then it dawned on me it was Women's Liberation Day. I glanced at the other courts. None of the wives was serving.

"Rose says I have to serve for her," Styron yelled. "She says all the women on the island have pledged not to serve today. They're sick and tired of being oppressed on the tennis court."

"All right," I said. "We'll serve for them if it means that much."

"We also want child-care centers on Martha's Vineyard," my wife said. "We're fed up with taking care of our children all day long."

"Can it wait until after the tennis game?" I asked.

Styron yelled across the net. "Rose says she won't

play the net unless women can have abortions any time they want them."

"It's OK with me," I said. "Are you ready?"

"I'm not going to play the back court," my wife said, "unless women have equal opportunity in jobs."

"You've got it," Styron said.

The game began grimly. I served to Rose who hit it out.

"Male chauvinist!" she screamed. Styron hit a smashing ball past my wife's ear, and my wife yelled "Sexist."

Despite their cursing, the women played extremely well. We discovered later that the Martha's Vineyard chapter of Women's Lib has advised all women playing tennis on Wednesday to pretend the tennis ball was their husband's head. It seemed to improve every woman's game.

Styron and I had to serve the entire three sets of tennis, and when we walked off the courts, the women were fresh as daisies.

"I want you to know," my wife said that evening as we were retiring, "I'm not a fanatic about women's lib. I'm prepared to fulfill my wifely duties."

"That's very decent of you," I said. "But it really doesn't matter because I'm too bushed from serving."

WOMEN'S LIBERATION

One of the many revolutions that has to be dealt with this year is the Women's Liberation Movement. Some men are treating it as a joke, but many men are taking it seriously.

My friend Rowland said to me the other evening at a bar in New York City, "I don't know what to do."

"Why?" I asked.

"I love my wife, but I believe in the Women's Liberation Movement."

"What do you mean?"

"Well, the women are right. They say that marriage is wrong and that no woman should be tied to any one man."

"Is that what they say?"

"Of course, and if you see it from their point of view, why should only one woman have access to me, when there are so many others that are just as deserving?"

"Rowland," I said, "are you sure that the Women's Liberation Movement was formed to share husbands?"

"Certainly. Most of us have been treating other women with benign neglect for years, and now we're paying the penalty. By maintaining the status quo at home, we have encouraged less fortunate women to radicalize and try to win, through revolution, what they couldn't win through elections. You can't blame them for wanting a piece of the action."

"You're a true liberal, Rowly," I said.

"I've become a realist," he said. "For years, like most married men, I was blinded to the oppression of women around me. I knew they were in chains, but I was afraid to speak up and to act on their behalf. I rationalized by saying, 'If I can keep my wife happy, I'm doing enough.' But I was living a lie. The only road to true equality is to make every woman happy, regardless of the sacrifices it entails."

"That's beautiful," I said.

"When women ask to be liberated," Rowland said, "they are asking to be treated as human beings, no more, no less. They want dignity, understanding and someone who cares. If that demands a revolution, then I say I will become part of their revolution."

"You're not advocating violence, are you?"

"I'm not for violence per se," Rowly said. "But if a woman becomes violent over me, I'm not going to turn her over to the authorities."

"I should hope not," I said. "How many women do you hope to liberate?"

"I'm not as young as I used to be," Rowland said, "but I'll liberate as many as the good Lord will let me."

"You're a saint, Rowland. A saint."

"I'm only doing what is right," he said modestly. "There comes a time in a man's life when he must stand up and be counted."

"Have you discussed this with your wife?"

"That's what I've been trying to tell you. I'm staying in town by myself tonight."

SEX AND THE
WASHINGTON MONUMENT

John Corry wrote a piece in *Harper's* magazine titled "Washington, Sex and Power." Corry's conclusions are that there is not as much sex in Washington as one might think, and while power acts as an aphrodisiac, more men in high positions get their kicks from politics than they do from bedfellows.

Corry says that Democrats are better Don Juans than Republicans, though some of the biggest lechers in Washington are middle-aged Republican conservatives, who were described by one hostess as "knee grabbers."

Corry says Southerners are better at horsing around than Northerners, and people who live in Georgetown are more interested in "what the kids are thinking" than having an affair with someone who lives in Bethesda, Maryland.

It is interesting to note that at the very time Corry was doing research on his piece for *Harper's,* a more in-depth study was being done by Professor Heinrich Applebaum for the National Institute of Domestic Affairs, otherwise known as NIDA (pronounced either "nee-da" or "negh-da" depending on how you feel at the time).

Professor Applebaum's study, titled "Sex and the Washington Monument," has come up with some startling revelations.

For one thing, there hasn't been one illicit affair in Washington since the Nixon administration took over. This compares favorably with the Johnson administration, when there were three, and the Kennedy administration, when there were four. (There were no statistics kept during the Eisenhower years.)

Applebaum indicates that there are several reasons for the lack of hanky-panky during the present regime.

230

One is that Attorney General John Mitchell's penchant for wiretapping has frightened off thousands of officials who had been thinking about it.

Another reason is the night sessions the Senate has been forced to hold because of the debate on the Cooper-Church Amendment. Ironically, this would have been a perfect excuse for Senators to engage in some extracurricular activity, except for the fact that they never knew when they would be called for a roll-call vote. It would be very hard to explain to their wives where they had been when the Washington *Post* reported the next morning that they were marked "absent."

Since this is an election year, House members have been so busy running for office they haven't had time to think about sex, Applebaum says. He also makes the point that most Congressmen are so strapped for cash they would rather put money in their campaign fund than spend it on some young secretary or passionate constituent.

As for the Executive branch, Applebaum's study revealed that Nixon appointees prefer watching spectator sports on TV rather than getting involved themselves.

Also, Applebaum points out, Nixon administration officials have been so drained trying to get through to someone in the White House each day that they're not good for much except to head home and go right to sleep.

The press and TV corps in Washington might have gotten into trouble, Applebaum notes, except for Spiro Agnew. The only thing the Vice President hasn't accused the press of, so far, is adultery. To keep Agnew from making such a charge, the entire membership of the National Press Club has taken a vow of chastity, which will remain in effect as long as the Vice President is in office.

If there has been any talk of sex in Washington, it's come from the Pentagon. Every time someone in Congress tries to cut the military budget, everyone in the Defense establishment starts screaming "Rape."

13

AND NOBODY LAUGHED

THE COMPUTER KNOWS ALL

Somewhere in this great land of ours there is a computer stashed full of information on you. Whenever you want a bank loan, a credit card or a job, this computer will, in a matter of seconds, give some total stranger almost every detail of your life.

Unfortunately for most of us, the computer is unable to discriminate between fact and malicious gossip, and once the information is fed into it, it stays there forever.

The other day I was considering going into a car pool with three other men, Hicks, Kroll, and Anderson. I have known these men casually for years, but when you join a car pool, you really want to know what they're like.

So I asked a friend of mine in the retail credit business if I could use his computer for a few hours.

He agreed, and I went down there and typed out: WHAT DO YOU KNOW ABOUT HICKS, AL, WHO LIVES AT 43 LOVER'S LEAP TERRACE?

The computer started chattering: HICKS, AL, BORN OCT. 23, 1925, BOTTLE-FED, BED-WETTER UNTIL 7 YEARS OLD.

I typed back: FORGET ABOUT CHILDHOOD AND GIVE ME SOME OTHER FACTS.

The computer replied: HICKS HAS A DOMINEERING WIFE WHO THE WHOLE WORLD THINKS IS AS SWEET AS MAPLE SYRUP. WHENEVER SHE GETS MAD AT HIM, HE STARTS BITING HIS NAILS.

I typed back: I'M NOT INTERESTED IN THAT. WHAT'S THE CONDITION OF HIS CAR?

The computer paused for a few seconds and then tapped out: HICKS OWNS 1957 BUICK CONVERTIBLE FOR WHICH HE IS STILL PAYING $80 A MONTH. IT HAS BEEN IN THE GARAGE 33 TIMES AND HAS COST HIM $1,500 IN REPAIRS. TWO OF THE SPRINGS IN THE BACK SEAT ARE BROKEN, AND HE NEEDS NEW SNOW TIRES. HE HAS THE CAR WASHED ONCE A MONTH.

It added: HICKS NEVER CHEATS ON HIS WIFE, THOUGH HE THINKS ABOUT IT A LOT.

THAT'S ENOUGH: I told the computer. NOW GIVE ME A RUNDOWN ON KROLL, H. G., WHO LIVES AT 1 LION'S DEN CIRCLE.

The tapes in the computer started turning furiously and finally stopped. The teletype began to chatter: KROLL, H. G., HAD STRONG MOTHER WHO DRESSED HIM IN SILK SAILOR SUITS UNTIL HE WAS 13 YEARS OLD.

GET ON WITH IT: I typed impatiently.

HE OWNS 1970 MERCURY FOUR-DOOR SEDAN WHICH HAS SPECIAL SILK SEAT COVERS. LIKES TO DRESS UP IN HIS WIFE'S CLOTHES WHEN CHILDREN ARE AT CAMP.

THAT'S ENOUGH: I typed angrily. WHAT ABOUT ANDERSON, E. L., 198 DOVER CLIFFS?

ANDERSON IS HAVING A BIG THING WITH A LADY COSMETICS BUYER FROM LORD & TAYLOR.

WHAT ABOUT HIS CAR? I demanded.

THEY DON'T USE HIS CAR. THEY USE HERS.

I DIDN'T MEAN THAT. IS HIS AUTOMOBILE SAFE FOR OUR CAR POOL?

IT IS NOW, BUT IF MRS. ANDERSON EVER FINDS OUT ABOUT THE LADY BUYER . . .

THANK YOU VERY MUCH: I typed. YOU'VE BEEN MOST HELPFUL.

DON'T MENTION IT. OH, BY THE WAY. WHEN ARE YOU GOING TO STOP BEATING YOUR WIFE?

YOU HAVE TO HAVE A SERVICE CONTRACT

In the world of planned obsolescence, the service contract plays a most vital role. There is hardly anything you can buy now that doesn't have a service contract to go with it.

The other day I went into my favorite department store to purchase a paper cup dispenser. It cost $1.50.

As the man was writing up the sales slip, he said, "Would you like to have a service contract with this?"

"What for?" I asked.

"Well, it could break down and you would have to call someone to fix it. If you take out a service contract, which will only cost you forty dollars for the year, we would send someone to your house free of charge."

"But why would you sell a paper cup dispenser that would break down in less than a year?"

"Please don't get me wrong. I'm not saying that this paper cup dispenser will break down. We've sold several of them that need no servicing at all. But our experience has been that the majority of the dispensers do cause trouble after frequent usage. Where did you intend to use this paper cup dispenser?"

"In the children's bathroom. They don't seem to ever rinse their glasses after they brush their teeth."

"Then you'll certainly need a service contract. These paper cup dispensers were not built to stand the punishment of children using them every day."

"But there is a guarantee with the paper cup dispenser."

"That's only if it's used by a senior citizen three times a week. Of course, you don't have to take the service contract—it's strictly optional.

"But we know a dentist who installed one of our paper cup dispensers in his office and it broke down. It kept dispensing three paper cups at one time. He didn't have a service contract, so it took three months before we could get to him. By the time our man repaired the dispenser, the dentist had used six hundred and forty-five dollars' worth of paper cups, not to mention the twenty-five dollars we had to charge him for the house call."

"But," I said naïvely, "it seems so unfair to sell someone a new product and then inform him it's liable to break down."

"On the contrary. We would be dishonest if we sold you the product and *didn't* inform you it would break down. These service contracts are for the protection of the customer. Two weeks ago a lady bought one of these paper cup dispensers and after two days, it wouldn't dispense any paper cups at all. She had to keep leaning over and trying to drink directly from the faucet. Fortunately, she had a service contract with us, and we sent over a man right away. It turned out a sprocket spring behind the reject lever had slipped out of the three-way hook. He

236

replaced it in an hour, and all the lady had to pay for was the new parts.

"Except for a bad back she developed trying to lean over the faucet, it only cost her twelve dollars."

"I still don't understand why a reliable store like this would carry a paper cup dispenser that won't hold up."

"Well, frankly, sir, we're not too fond of these paper cup dispensers ourselves. We don't even make any money on them."

"Then why do you sell them?" I asked angrily.

"Because," he said primly, "we make all our profit on the service contract, stupid."

THE NO KNOCK ON THE DOOR

There was a shoot-out in Phoenix which had national implications. The police, taking advantage of a "no-knock" law, raided a house where they suspected hippies had narcotics. Unfortunately, at the time of the raid the hippies had moved out and a married couple had moved in. Since the raid took place at 1:30 in the morning, the husband refused to believe the men were police and shot one. He, in turn, was shot. The police sergeant said after the raid, "It was a misunderstanding. The couple probably felt they were defending their home against some hippies, and the officers thought they were fighting some criminals."

Now, opponents of the "no-knock" law have always claimed the big danger of it was that if the police enter someone's home without knocking, they could get shot.

Since the Constitution permits you to defend your own home, it is possible that more policemen will be shot than narcotics will be found.

This will make the cops uptight, and so, to protect themselves, they'll start shooting first, and before you know it, there will be bloodbaths all over the country.

The reason law enforcement officials say they need the "no-knock" law is if they knock first, the suspects inside the house will flush narcotics evidence down the toilet. Only a strong "no-knock" law, they claim, can prevent anyone from dashing to the bathroom.

This sounds reasonable, but, as we have seen in Phoenix, it can only lead to a shoot-out because the people inside the house can never be certain that the people crashing into their home are policemen.

There is a solution to this problem which we think could satisfy the law-and-order people, as well as the innocent home owner.

I am proposing that the "no-knock" law be stricken from the books and replaced with a "no-flush" law.

This is how it would work: The police would still have to get a warrant to enter someone's home. They would also have to knock before entering. But if it were a narcotics or gambling raid, they would have to shout at the top of their voices, *"This is a raid. Anyone who flushes the toilet will be arrested."*

One policeman would be stationed by the water meter nearest the house or apartment to monitor any fluctuation in water pressure during the raid.

When the police enter the apartment, they will have the authority to check the bathrooms. If anyone flushes during the raid, he will be assumed to have committed a crime, and this evidence will be accepted by the court as prima-facie evidence of guilt.

The "no-flush" law may be considered by civil libertarians as an invasion of privacy, but it is certainly more acceptable than a "no-knock" law, and safer, too.

I made this suggestion at an annual meeting of the American Bar Association in St. Louis, but they only laughed at me.

So I've decided to take my case to the public. Would you rather have the police crash in on you at one o'clock in the morning without warning? Or would you rather first hear a knock on the door and give up your bathroom privileges while they're searching through your home?

AFFLUENCE IS NO FUN

One of the troubles with an affluent society is that the more affluent everyone gets, the less anyone wants to do.

This is particularly true when it comes to plumbers, electricians and other members of the establishment.

I knew electricians and plumbers were doing well, but I didn't know how well until my air-conditioning unit broke over the weekend. I called the company that installed it, and instead of a live voice, a recording started, "This is the Affluent Heating and Air-Conditioning Company. All our plumbers have gone to Southampton for the weekend. If you have any problems with your air conditioning, leave a message—after you hear the beep—and we will try to get to you by Labor Day."

It wasn't very encouraging, but I left my name, address and telephone number. Nothing happened for three days, so I decided to call back. A secretary answered the phone.

"My air conditioner's broken. Could you send somebody over to fit it?" She started laughing.

"What's so blasted funny?" I demanded.

"All our men are finished for the day."

"But it's only two o'clock in the afternoon," I said.

"Well, they started at nine this morning," she replied.

"But even the banks stay open longer than that," I yelled.

"The banks don't have unions," she said.

"Listen, lady, this is an emergency. Couldn't you find someone to come over and fix it tomorrow morning?"

"That's impossible," she said.

"Why?"

"Our plumbers don't like to make house calls. Now, if you'd like to bring your air conditioner into the office, we might have our resident plumber look at it."

"But it's a big mother of an air conditioner," I protested.

"That's all right. Shall I put you down for Thursday at nine o'clock?"

Thursday I rented a station wagon and two friends helped me put the air conditioner in. I carried it into the waiting room, where there were thirty people sitting on straight-backed chairs with their air conditioners on their laps.

"Is this your first visit?" the lady in uniform asked, as I wiped the perspiration off my forehead.

"Yes," I said.

"That will be thirty dollars for an office visit. If you have to come back, it will only be twenty-five dollars a visit." She gave me a number and said I would be called.

At 12:30 my number was called.

I was ushered into the plumber's office. He was on the phone to his broker. "I told you to buy ten thousand shares of IBM, not ITT. Call me back."

He made me sit down, and then he knelt over my air conditioner. In a few minutes he said, "Mr. Buchwald, you have a very sick air conditioner here."

"I know that. Do something," I pleaded.

"The only plumber who specializes in this type of air conditioner is in Europe on his yacht for the summer."

"Then there's no hope?"

He shook his head. "Had you called us sooner. . . ."

I took the air conditioner home and put it in the back-yard.

That night, after the children had gone to sleep, I went outside and shot it. I buried it next to a broken hot water heater that had expired last winter, the last time the plumber wouldn't come. I know they'll be happy together.

THE POTHOLE CONVENTION

I just finished attending a pothole convention in Pittsburgh, Pennsylvania. Pothole makers from all over the world jammed the city's hotels and motels, and officials of the National Pothole Association said it was the most successful meeting they ever had.

Hiram H. Patches, president of the NPA, said, "Thanks to a very bad winter, pothole production has tripled.

We've had potholes where we've never had potholes before. At one time you only saw potholes in the poorer neighborhoods and on unpaved streets. But now, because of new technological breakthroughs, you'll find potholes on paved suburban roads, as well as highways and bridges. We can't keep up with the demand."

Mr. Patches took me to the exhibition hall, where equipment, as well as designs for potholes, was on display.

"Most potholes used to be rectangular, but we're getting demands for potholes in every shape and form. This kidney-shaped one is very popular, and this oval one has been moving quite well, and this zigzag pothole is a winner."

"You mean you can deliver a pothole made to order?"

"Of course. When you have a pothole on a highway or a main street, you don't want one that looks ugly and doesn't fit in with the landscape."

"How do you make a pothole?" I asked.

"It's very complicated," Mr. Patches said, "and there are many methods. The old-fashioned way of making a pothole was to dig up a street and then fill it in again with a cheaper subsurface material. Before the material hardened, you would send a truck over it and it would make a pothole any size you wanted.

"But the difficulty with this method was that it was too expensive to dig up the streets just to make a pothole. So our research people attacked the problem. They discovered that if you use a cheap asphalt or a thin tar surface on the roads, all you need to make a good-sized pothole are enough vehicles passing over it. Now most of our potholes are made by using cheaper material and bad labor."

"What kind of pothole makers are those?" I asked, pointing to a very interesting display which showed what happens to the chassis of a car that hits a pothole.

"That's our freeze-and-thaw breaker. We have discovered that by freezing a road or highway to zero temperature, and then thawing it, you can make potholes automatically. The size depends on how many heavy trucks and busses roll over the surface.

"We can make a pothole with an automobile as well, but it takes twice as long as it does with a good solid truck."

We walked along and came to a theater where I noticed someone getting an award. "What's going on?"

"Every year, to publicize potholes, we give an award to the city that has the most potholes. Pittsburgh won this year, though I must say it was close: New York, Chicago, Cleveland and Detroit are all protesting that they should have got the prize."

"There seems to be a great market for potholes. Who buys them?"

"Our biggest customers are elected officials."

"I don't understand."

"Most politicians, particularly those up for election, want to do something for the people. So they order the potholes from us. Once they've been installed, the voters complain about them and then the officials arrange for the potholes to be filled in. This way the politicians win the undying gratitude of the electorate."

"So, without your potholes it would be impossible for anyone to run for reelection in the United States?"

"Exactly. Look, there's Mayor Daley ordering a gross of potholes for the Loop."

JUNK INSTEAD OF JUNK MAIL

A lot of people are being shaken up these days by receiving unsolicited plastic credit cards. In the past the consumer had the option whether to ask for credit or not. But now, in the great battle for the hearts and dollars of the American customer, the banks, oil companies and hotel chains are shoving their credit cards at you whether you want them or not.

It isn't just the specter of a wife or teen-ager receiving a credit card and going berserk that bothers most American breadwinners. It's the principle of the thing, and where will it all end? What is to prevent a company that sends unsolicited credit cards to your home from sending merchandise instead?

I don't believe it is too farfetched to see this happening in a few years.

You come home, and there on your front lawn is a complete dining room set with table, twelve chairs and cabinet. Attached to leg of the table is a note:

GREETINGS:

We are happy to inform you that we consider you an excellent credit risk, and, to show our faith in you, we are leaving this dining room set on your lawn. Our credit reports on you indicate that you favor Colonial furniture, and we have chosen this particular mahogany wood which we know will go well with the rest of your furnishings. If for some reason this particular dining room set does not meet your requirements, you may return it to our warehouse within ten days, and you will not be charged for it. If it is not returned, we will assume that we made the right choice, and we shall start billing you monthly.

Or you could wake up in the morning and find parked outside your door a new "fire eater," with the following letter taped to the windshield:

CONGRATULATIONS:

You are now the owner of a new "fire eater," the fastest, most comfortable, economical automobile on the road. Because of your high credit rating, we have taken the liberty of registering this car in your name with the State Vehicle Bureau.

If for any reason you change your mind and decide you don't want to be one of the with-it people call this number and we will have the car taken away, at no cost to you, except for the towing charges.

Also, if you do not accept this exceptional buy, you must go down to the State Vehicle Bureau and inform them of this decision. Otherwise we will start charging you interest beginning next week.

The final indignity would be to receive a registered letter from a development company which read:

DEAR SIR:

We're happy to inform you that you are now the proud owner of a new ranch house in Paradise Acres. This extra-ordinary home (the deed is enclosed) has three bedrooms, two and half baths, a playroom and completely equipped kitchen and will be ready for you to move into within two weeks.

A check on your credit rating shows that you can easily afford this remarkable buy, and we have taken the liberty of deducting from your bank account the small down payment.

If we don't hear from you by registered mail within the next thirty-six hours, we will assume that you will be joining us at Paradise Acres. On the other hand, if you return the deed, then we ask you to contact our lawyers so some equitable arrangement can be worked out for our time and inconvenience.

Cheers.

THE GREAT DATA FAMINE

One of the major problems we face in the 1970's is that so many computers will be built in the next decade that there will be a shortage of data to feed them.

Professor Heinrich Applebaum, director of the Computer Proliferation Center at Grogbottom, has voiced concern about the crisis and has urged a crash program to produce enough data to get our computers through the seventies.

"We didn't realize," the professor told me, "that computers would absorb so much information in such a fast period of time. But if our figures are correct, every last bit of data in the world will have been fed into a machine by January twelfth, 1976, and an information famine will follow, which could spread across the world."

"It sounds serious," I said.

"It is serious," he replied. "Man has created his own

monster. He never realized when he invented the computer that there would not be enough statistics to feed it. Even now, there are some computers starving to death because there is no information to put into them. At the same time, the birth rate of computers is increasing by thirty percent a year. Barring some sort of worldwide holocaust, we may soon have to find data for thirty million computers, with new ones being born every day."

"You make it sound so frightening."

"It is frightening," Professor Applebaum said. "The new generation of computers is more sophisticated than the older generation, and the computers will refuse to remain idle just because there is nothing to compute, analyze or calculate. Left to their own devices, the Lord only knows what they will do."

"Is there any solution, Professor?"

"New sources of data must be found. The government must expand, and involved studies must be thought up to make use of the computers' talents. The scientific community, instead of trying to solve problems with computers, must work on finding problems for the computers to solve."

"Even if the scientists really don't want the answers?"

"Naturally. The scientific community invented the computer. Now it must find ways of feeding it. I do not want to be an alarmist, but I can see the day coming when millions of computers will be fighting for the same small piece of data, like savages."

"Is there any hope that the government will wake up to the data famine in time?"

"We have a program ready to go as soon as the bureaucrats in Washington give us the word. We are recommending that no computer can be plugged in more than three hours a day.

"We are also asking the government for fifty billion dollars to set up data-manufacturing plants all over the country. This data mixed with soybeans could feed hundreds of thousands of computer families for months.

"And finally we are advocating a birth control program for computers. By forcing a computer to swallow a small bit of erroneous information, we could make it sterile forever, and it would be impossible for it to reproduce any more of its kind."

"Would you advocate abortions for computers?" I asked Applebaum.

"Only if the Vatican's computer gives us its blessing."

MY NAME'S HOWARD

Every man has one big dream in him that keeps him going for all of his life. My dream is quite a simple one:

I'm taking an airplane from Las Vegas to Paradise Island in the Bahamas, and sitting next to me is a gaunt, thin man with a mustache. He is wearing a white shirt open at the collar, an old sweater, an unpressed pair of slacks and tennis sneakers.

"Hi," I say in my dream, sticking out my hand, "my name is Art."

He refuses to shake hands but mutters, "My name is Howard."

"Howard what?" I ask, trying to be friendly.

"Just Howard," he snarls. "Now if you don't mind, I have private detective reports to read."

"What business are you in, Howard?"

"A little bit of this, a little bit of that. I buy and sell states," he said.

"You mean estates, don't you?"

"I said states, and I mean states." He is becoming angry again.

I try to get on his good side. "You seen any good movies lately?"

"The only movie I've seen lately is *The Outlaw* with Jane Russell."

"Oh? How did you like it?"

"I think it's one of the greatest films ever made," Howard says.

"So do I," I tell him.

"You do?" For the first time he smiles.

"Yes, sir. It's been twenty years and I still can't get Jane Russell's performance out of my mind."

I can see Howard is starting to warm up.

"I was hoping they'd show it on this flight," he says confidentially.

"Wouldn't that be something," I say.

We have nothing to talk about for a few minutes, and then I say, "What do you think of Las Vegas?"

"It's a nice place to own, but I wouldn't want to live there," he replies.

"That's a good one," I say, slapping Howard's knee. "Where do you stay in Las Vegas?"

"I have the choice of many hotels, but I usually stay at the Desert Inn on the top floor because I like the view."

"Do you gamble?"

"Sort of, but I never go near the tables," he says.

"That's a good idea," I say. "Stick with the slot machines and they can't hurt you."

We lapsed into silence again. I notice Howard is writing notes on yellow legal-size pads. Then he crushes up a page and starts all over.

"Having trouble?" I ask.

"I'm trying to fire a guy, and I don't know how to say it in a nice way."

By this time our plane is landing in Nassau. While I'm gathering up my things, Howard dashes off the plane. I notice he has left his briefcase behind.

I try to run after him, but he has already jumped into a limousine.

"Howard, Howard," I yell, "you forgot your briefcase."

"I don't need it," he yells as the limo pulls out. "You can have it."

I open the briefcase when I get to my hotel room and, to my surprise and joy, find $100,000,000, all in new 1,000-dollar bills.

THE CURSE IS WORKING

There is a great deal of soul-searching going on in this

country as to why things have gone wrong. The Democrats blame the Republicans. The Republicans blame the radical-liberals. The students blame the establishment. The establishment blames Dr. Spock.

The one thing everyone seems in agreement on is that we're in a mess. The only thing no one is in agreement on is how we got into it.

I can now reveal the exact date and hour when things started going downhill in the United States. I can also reveal, for the first time, the reason why.

On November 10, 1958, at 11 A.M., a small brown package insured for $1,000,000 was delivered to the Smithsonian Institution. Inside was the famous Hope diamond, a gift to the United States from Harry Winston, one of America's famous jewelers.

The Smithsonian was thrilled to have such a beautiful stone to display to the public. But what the American officials did not take into consideration was that the diamond had a curse on it—it brings bad luck to anyone who owns it.

Here are just a few of the things that happened to people who possessed the Hope diamond:

Louis XIV gave it to his mistress, Mme. de Montespan, and immediately abandoned her. The king himself contracted an incurable disease and finished his reign in disgrace.

The beautiful Princess Lamballe wore the diamond and was beaten to death by a mob during the French Revolution. Her head was paraded before Marie Antoinette, her closest friend. King Louis XVI, who inherited the stone, and his lovely Marie didn't fare any better.

The diamond was missing for several years. Then it turned up in the possession of Wilhelm Fals, a Dutch diamond cutter. Fals died of grief when his son Hendrik stole it from him. Hendrik committed suicide.

François Beaulieu, a Frenchman who owned it next, died of starvation after selling it to an Englishman, David Eliason, who sold it to an Irishman named Henry Thomas Hope.

The diamond was sold at auction to Jacques Celot, a
248

jeweler who went insane and committed suicide. A Russian prince, Ivan Kanitovski, also owned it at one time. He was, as everyone knows, stabbed to death. Catherine the Great is said to have worn the diamond, and she died of apoplexy.

After that, it was just one bad-luck story after another. One of the female owners, after living high on the hog, was reduced to working as a scrubwoman for two dollars a day in a shipyard.

A Spanish owner drowned in a shipwreck. A Greek broker who sold it to a Turkish sultan was killed with his entire family when his car went over a precipice in the mountains. When the sultan gave the gem to his favorite wife, she stabbed him. The McLean family, who owned the diamond before Winston, didn't come out of it too well, either.

The Hope diamond has brought nothing but grief to its owners, and whoever accepted it on behalf of the United States in 1958 did this country a great disservice.

Anyone who recalls what went on before 1958 and compares it to what is going on now knows we made a mistake.

The question is: What is the solution?

One suggestion is that we present the Hope diamond as a gift to the Soviet Union. President Nixon could drop it off on his next trip to Europe.

If the Soviets refuse to accept it, there's always the Red Chinese. What better way of showing we want to be friends with the Chinese than to give it to Mrs. Mao Tse-tung to wear in her navel at the next rally at Peking Square?

Write your Congressman before it's too late!

ON BUYING A FLAG

There's much more to buying an American flag these days than people think.

I discovered this when I went into a store to purchase a flag to fly on the Fourth of July, which Bob Hope and the Nixon administration have declared a Republican national holiday.

The salesman said he was hard put to keep flags in stock. "I owe it all to television," he said. "Every time one of the major news programs films one of the freaks burning the American flag, we sell out. What can I do for you?"

"I'd like to buy an American flag."

"Good for you, sir. Show those lousy peace people what you think of them."

"Well, I, uh-uh—"

"Would you like it for light combat or heavy fighting?"

"I beg your pardon?"

"We have this model here which is very popular with the hard hats. The bottom part of the pole is tipped in metal so when you hit someone with it, it doesn't crack."

"I hadn't really thought to—"

"Now this model over here, while slightly more expensive, is perfect for close hand-to-hand combat. The eagle on the top of the pole has been made especially sharp so when you lunge with it, you can really do damage to the groin. . . ."

"That's very nice, but—"

"Here's an all-metal pole. It's much harder than the wooden one, and you can really get someone in the shins with it."

"Look, I—"

"This is our shorty. The pole is half the regular size, so it can be used as a club instead of a lance. Many of our customers like to get in the thick of it and swing wildly. The hard hats had great success with it in St. Louis when they beat up a woman and her veteran son."

"It's a beauty," I said, "but I was hoping that you would have a—"

"This one here is heavier in weight, and you can swing it like a baseball bat. Feel the grip on it. It will never fly out of your hands."

"I was looking for something less expensive."

"We have the mighty midget over here. It's only two

feet long, and while it looks fragile, you can really do damage with it."

"All right. I'll take a mighty midget."

"Very good, sir. Do you have any identification with you?"

"Identification?"

"Yes, sir. We always ask for identification. Do you have any proof you support President Nixon's policies in Cambodia?"

"Well, I don't have it on me. I didn't know you needed proof of that to buy an American flag."

"Of course you do. The American flag is a very lethal weapon and we don't sell it to any stranger who just comes in off the street."

"I'm sorry. I should have brought some identification with me."

"Why did you want it in the first place?"

"Well, if you don't tell anyone," I said, "I was going to hang it out my window on the Fourth of July, to protect my home."

THE NEW GAME, DEPRESSION

The latest parlor game to catch on in the United States is called Depression. Not since charades took the country by storm has there been anything to compare with Depression. The object of the game, which can be played indoors and out, at cocktail parties, dinners, soda fountains or any other place, is to depress the other person more than he depresses you.

Most readers have been playing the game without even realizing it.

This is how it goes:

Jones, at a cocktail party, serves: "I've never seen the country in worse shape."

Evans returns serve: "The kids just don't give a damn about anything."

Jones hits it back: "They have no respect and no values."

251

Evans at the net: "If they didn't have everything handed to them on a platter, they wouldn't be so ready to attack the system."

Jones, aiming for the sidelines: "They ought to get some education before they start telling us how to run things."

Evans, making a great save: "What they need is a haircut and a bath."

Jones lobs it back: "They want to talk, but they won't listen."

Evans returns it: "We're in a helluva mess."

Jones swings and misses: "You can say that again."

Evans won the game because he depressed Jones more than Jones depressed him. But it was very close.

Depression has also become the most popular game with college and high school students. Here's a mixed-doubles match at a coffeehouse.

Sophomore serves: "I've never seen the country in worse shape."

Junior retrieves it: "Nobody understands us."

Sophomore's date: "I can't stand talking to my parents anymore."

Junior's date returns ball: "All they can think about is money, money, money."

Sophomore returns with backhand: "We have nothing to live for."

Junior slams it back: "We can't make any plans for the future."

Sophomore's date runs for the ball: "Nobody gives a damn about us."

Junior's date in backcourt: "Nobody loves us."

Sophomore hits it back: "All they can say is 'Get a haircut.' "

Junior returns it: "They're all hypocrites."

Sophomore's date: "I wish I were dead."

Junior's date: "I wish I were more dead than you were dead."

Sophomore: "We're all going to be dead whether we want to be or not."

Junior: "Oh, obscenity."

This match happened to be a tie, so it was agreed the couples would have a play-off the following evening at the same time.

While the game is being played all over the United States (Will we ever forget those matches on Wall Street), Washington is still considered the superbowl of Depression, and you can't go anywhere in this town without someone wanting to play.

If someone tries to get you depressed about the war, you can get him depressed about inflation. And if he attempts to get you depressed about dissent, you can get him depressed about the administration.

There are so many subjects to choose from in Washington that it's getting almost impossible to depress somebody more than he depresses you.

TODAY LAOS, TOMORROW . . .

Whenever something new happens in the war in Indochina, I always seek out my dear friend Joseph Wallstop, the dean of the hawk columnists.

Late last fall, as the war was winding down, Joe had become more and more depressed, so I didn't know what mood I'd find him in. Happily, when I went down to his war room, located in the basement of his house, I found him dancing a jig.

"Joe," I said, "you're your old self again."

"They've finally listened to me," Joe said gleefully. "I've wanted to invade Laos for four years."

"That's wonderful, Joe," I said. "It must be great to see a dream come true."

"I didn't think President Nixon had the guts," Joe said. "But, thank God, he has finally bought my plan. Hanoi will be on the ropes in a matter of weeks."

"I thought you told everyone Hanoi was on the ropes after the Tet offensive."

"They *were* on the ropes," Joe said. "But *they* didn't know it. I still maintain the Tet offensive was the biggest allied victory of the war."

"Bigger than the invasion of Cambodia?" I said.

"Cambodia was different. In Cambodia, I wiped out all the Communist sanctuaries that were supplying the Reds in South Vietnam."

"But if you wiped out all the Communist sanctuaries, why did you have to go into Laos?"

"Because, you idiot, Hanoi is hurting, so they're sending everything down the Ho Chi Minh Trail. Once I interdict the Ho Chi Minh Trail, I'll have the Commies on the ropes again."

"Unless they think of something else," I said.

"Come over here," Joe said. He took me over to a very large table which had a relief map of Southeast Asia on it. He had flags all over it: green for allied troops, red for Communist troops and blue for American aircraft. He even had a miniature Sixth Fleet which he could push around the table.

He put on his campaign hat and said: "This is what I want to do: I want to bomb everything in Cambodia and Laos. That may force Hanoi to send their stuff through Thailand."

"Why, it's the old interdiction ploy," I said.

"Exactly. This will give me an excuse to invade Thailand. Once I'm in Thailand, I'll give General Abrams time to shape up the South Vietnamese army so they can invade North Vietnam."

Joe moved the green flags across the DMZ.

"You mean you're going to invade North Vietnam?"

"What choice do I have?" Joe replied. "Once I clean out the sanctuaries in North Vietnam, Hanoi will be on the ropes."

"So they'll sue for peace?" I said excitedly.

"No, they won't," he said disgustedly. "They'll ask the Chinese to intervene."

"Joe," I said nervously, "you're moving the green flags up to the Chinese border. You're not thinking of sending the South Vietnamese into China?"

"Why not?" said Joe. "That's where all the supplies are coming from."

A red phone in the corner rang urgently and Joe picked

it up. "Yes, Mr. President. You're doing fine. Just fine. Once you secure the Ho Chi Minh Trail, call me back and I'll tell you what to do next."

AND NOBODY LAUGHED

The last person to laugh in the United States was Robert Ketchum on Monday, August 3, 1978. There was no law passed to prevent people from laughing; they just quit voluntarily.

No one knows exactly when people gave up laughing in America. The Republicans claimed it was during the Johnson administration, and the Democrats said it happened during President Nixon's term in office. Putnam Toynbee, who in 1984 wrote *The Definitive History of the Seventies,* claims the first culture group to give up laughing was students.

"There's nothing to laugh about," they said to each other in despair. "Everything is rotten. The government, the establishment, the system and life itself. We're doomed to a plastic existence, and we'll be damned if we're going to laugh about it. If we show in any way we're happy, it will be a sign of weakness."

Toynbee points out that anything youth did in the United States was eventually picked up by the adult population, and when young people stopped laughing, older people started to emulate them.

Scowling became very fashionable in the with-it crowd. Articles began appearing in the chic magazines that laughter was out. Pretty soon the word had filtered to the hinterlands that anyone who laughed about anything was a fool or a knave.

Advertisers, sensitive to the mood of the consumer, canceled all comedy shows on television; the networks put out memos ordering all laughter bleeped from their programs, and newspapers dropped any stories or comic strips which might produce a chuckle for the reader.

Toynbee says in his book that it was difficult for a certain segment of society to give up laughing, but these people did it privately in their homes, where no one could see them.

A group of friends would get together, send the children off for the night with relatives, and then laugh for two or three hours among themselves.

There were certain key clubs where people could go to hear a comedian or see a funny motion picture from the past. But as the older generation started dying out, the clubs went bankrupt, as there were no young laughers to take their place.

Laughter in public buildings was forbidden and considered exceptionally bad taste. Anyone who laughed in a restaurant or theater was asked to leave.

If someone attempted to laugh on the street or in a park, he was met with stony stares or assaulted by angry passersby.

The government contributed to the antilaughter campaign by issuing pronouncements every day that things were worse than they were the day before.

To make sure that people wouldn't go back to their old ways, Washington raised taxes, passed outrageous laws, told of international threats, and gave out grim economic reports. Life indeed presented a dismal picture.

Toynbee claims the last person in the United States known to have laughed in public was Robert Ketchum, who lived in Salem, Massachusetts.

Ketchum was standing on a street corner when a friend of his, Adolph Green, walked by and slid on a banana peel. Before he realized what he was doing, Ketchum burst into laughter.

An angry crowd gathered and grabbed Ketchum and dragged him to the center of the square, where they tied him to a post, threw branches from trees at his feet, and burned him at the stake. All three networks covered the event, and the lesson was not lost on the populace. Toynbee feels it will be some time before anyone laughs in public in the United States again.